# Shrubs and Trees
# of the Sout

written by
Janice Emily Bowers

illustrations by
Brian Wignall

Editorial: T.J. Priehs, Ron Foreman
Design: Christina Watkins
Production: TypeWorks
Printing: Lorraine Press, Inc.

221 North Court
Tucson, Arizona 85701

# Contents

COVER: Creosote bush, *Larrea tridentata*. Photo by Jeff Gnass.

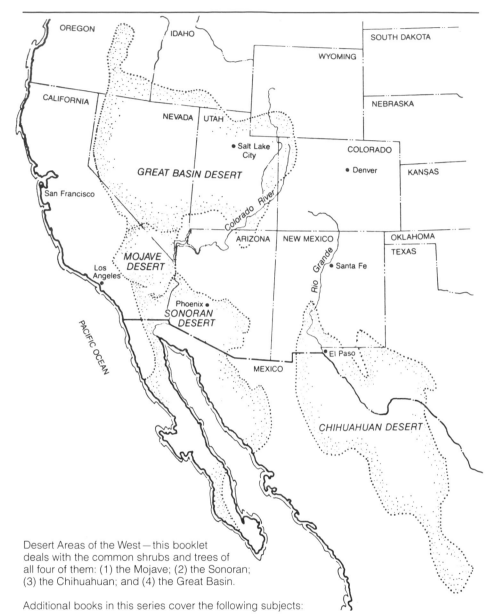

Desert Areas of the West — this booklet
deals with the common shrubs and trees of
all four of them: (1) the Mojave; (2) the Sonoran;
(3) the Chihuahuan; and (4) the Great Basin.

Additional books in this series cover the following subjects:

*Shrubs and Trees of the Southwest Uplands*, ISBN Number 0-911408-41-X. Shrubs and trees of
the drainages of the upper portion of the Rio Grande and Pecos rivers; and by the Colorado River
south of Grand Junction, Colorado, and its tributaries the Gunnison, San Juan, and Little Colorado.
A 4,500-foot contour has been selected as defining the beginning of the Uplands.

*Flowers of the Southwest Mountains*, ISBN Number 0-911408-61-4. Mountain flowers of Arizona,
New Mexico, Colorado, and Utah, starting at 7,000 feet in the Transition Life Zone.

*Flowers of the Southwest Deserts*, ISBN Number 0-911408-65-7. Flowers of the Chihuahuan, Sonoran, and Mojave deserts.

# The Setting

Deserts are regions of scanty and irregular rainfall. In the arid southwestern corner of North America, rainfall varies from a few inches to as much as nine or ten annually. Some years more than the average might fall; other years, rain is almost nonexistent. One result of scanty and sporadic rainfall is that permanent water is rare in deserts: springs are few, and most streambeds are dry except after heavy rains. Desert summers are notoriously hot, yet winters often bring freezing nights. Air temperatures fluctuate greatly over a twenty-four-hour period, especially in the winter, when a difference of forty degrees between day and night is not uncommon.

In the greater Southwest, a vast desert extends from southeastern California to western Texas, and from central Utah and parts of adjacent states, to the Mexican states of Baja California, Sonora, Chihuahua, and Coahuila. Biologists and geographers generally recognize four sub-regions within this great, arid tract: these are the Mojave, Sonoran, Chihuahuan, and Great Basin deserts. Each has a characteristic climate and a distinct assemblage of plants and animals.

The largest desert in the Southwest, the Chihuahuan Desert, covers more than 200,000 square miles in northeastern Mexico, western Texas, southern New Mexico, and southeastern Arizona. The Chihuahuan Desert lies at moderately high elevations compared to the other deserts: 2,000–5,000 feet above sea level in its northern part and from 5,000–6,000 feet in the southern part. Winter temperatures are low, and freezing weather occasionally lasts for several days. Rain falls mostly in the summer as local, drenching thunderstorms. Throughout much of the region, runoff drains not into rivers but into basins enclosed by hills and mountain ranges. Characteristic Chihuahuan Desert plants include tarbush, creosote bush, white thorn, guayule, and candelilla.

The Great Basin Desert, a close second in size to the Chihuahuan Desert, covers nearly 190,000 square miles. Much of Nevada and Utah are in the Great Basin Desert, as are parts of Oregon, Washington, Idaho, and Wyoming. This desert is characterized by interior drainage basins. The desert floor is broken by hundreds of mountain ranges, the highest reaching 14,246 feet above sea level. Lying in the rain shadow of the Sierra Nevada-Cascade chain, the Great Basin Desert receives from four to twelve inches of precipitation annually, about half in winter, half in summer. In this cold desert, winters always bring freezing temperatures and snow. Characteristic Great Basin desert plants are rubber rabbitbrush, big sagebrush, shadscale, and blackbrush.

The Sonoran Desert comprises 120,000 square miles of arid mountains and plains in northwestern Mexico, southern Arizona, and southeastern California. The warmest of the four deserts, the Sonoran Desert seldom if ever experiences freezing temperatures for longer than twenty-four hours. Summer temperatures are typically among the highest in the United States: daily highs of 120 degrees F or more are not uncommon in the western half of the desert. Elevations range from below sea level to 4,500 feet. Precipitation averages less than two to about twelve inches annually, depending on elevation, with well-defined winter and summer rainy seasons. Saguaro, blue paloverde, littleleaf paloverde, triangle-leaf bursage, ironwood, jumping cholla, and creosote bush are some of the many characteristic Sonoran Desert plants.

The Mojave Desert, which covers about 35,000 square miles, is the smallest North American desert and lies largely in southeastern California and southern Nevada. Elevations range from 280 feet below sea level to about 4,000 feet above sea level. Coming mostly in autumn and winter, rainfall averages three to four inches per year across the desert floor. With rising elevation, this increases to about eleven inches annually. The hottest temperature ever recorded in the United States — 134 degrees F — was logged in the Mojave Desert at Death Valley. During the summer, temperatures often exceed 100 degrees F. Winters are colder than in the Sonoran Desert: in valley bottoms, where cold air settles at night, temperatures may drop below zero degrees F in the winter. Characteristic Mojave Desert plants include white bursage, creosote bush, Joshua tree, and indigo bush.

# The Plants

The harshness of the desert climate inevitably means that desert plant life is stringent rather than lush. In many parts of the desert, rocks rather than vegetation dominate the landscape. Even so, the variety of desert trees, shrubs and wildflowers may astonish visitors from moister regions. About twenty-seven hundred species of plants are known from the Sonoran Desert alone. Desert floras include not only representatives of the Cactus and Agave families, as one might expect, but also members of the Rose and Buttercup families, which is, perhaps, less predictable. Given permanent water, even members of the Elm, Willow, and Sycamore families can survive in the southwestern deserts. This book describes and illustrates most of the common trees and shrubs of our southwestern deserts and includes a few others that, while uncommon, are worth knowing.

Unlike desert wildflowers, which germinate and bloom during the brief rainy seasons and leave their seeds to endure the harshest times, desert trees and shrubs must adapt to the climate year-round. Their modifications may be eye-catching, like the water-swollen stems of certain cacti, such as the saguaro and barrel cactus. Other adaptations, although less striking, are equally effective: the tiny, drought-deciduous leaves characteristic of paloverde, for instance, or the furry, gray leaves of brittlebush.

Many desert shrubs dispense with leaves altogether, relying instead on green stems for photosynthesis, yet others, like bitter condalia, do not. One explanation for this apparent paradox is that desert climates are wildly erratic. Where the climate is more predictable, the dominant plants tend to converge on a similar plant form: chaparral plants with their small, tough leaves are a good example. But in deserts, the fluctuating climate discourages this kind of convergence. Strategies that work in some years might fail in others. A summer might be so hot, for example, that the succulents literally cook to death. A drought might be so prolonged that drought-deciduous shrubs die before they recover from dormancy. Deserts, therefore, are places where plant strategies — thus a variety of plant forms — accumulate. The desert embraces leafless shrubs like crucifixion thorn as well as leafy ones like bitter condalia. Each represents a different accommodation to the unpredictable arid environment.

The desert environment poses special problems for cacti. One of these is heat. Most leafy plants cool themselves during the day by opening their pores. The movement of water from stem to leaf to air keeps leaf temperatures from rising too high. Because their pores open only at night, cacti cannot take advantage of such transpirational cooling. They adapt to desert heat by internal mechanisms. Teddybear cholla, for instance, can withstand an air temperature of 138 degrees F. Most other plants would literally cook at this temperature. In the summertime, the internal temperature of teddybear cholla often rises 59 degrees F or more above the air temperature.

# How to Use This Book

The difference between a tree and a shrub, especially in a region where few trees exceed thirty or forty feet in height, is qualitative rather than quantitative. Generally, trees are single-stemmed, while shrubs are many-stemmed. Some species, however, such as the honey mesquite, are shrubby in certain habitats and arborescent, or treelike, in others. And, while we usually think of shrubs as being relatively short-lived, some desert shrubs may live for hundreds of years, as long as any desert tree.

The trees and shrubs depicted in this book are grouped by flower color: green or otherwise inconspicuous; white or creamy; yellow or orange; red, pink, or magenta; blue, lavender, or purple.

For every plant, both a common name and a scientific name are given. Though common names (like creosote bush and barrel cactus) can be delightfully descriptive, they are completely unstandardized. Most plants lack widely accepted common names. A few, however, possess several. To add to the confusion, some quite different plants share the same common name. Fortunately, every plant has only one valid scientific name which is shared by no other plant.

Scientific names, composed from Latin or Greek roots, have three parts. The first part, the genus name, corresponds roughly to your family name. The second part, the species name, is equivalent to your first, or given, name. Just as your given name distinguishes you from other members of your immediate family, so the species distinguishes a plant from every other species in the genus. The third part of every plant name is the authority — the surname of the botanist who first described the plant as a new species. If later botanists transfer the species into a different genus, their names become part of the authority, too. Often these surnames are abbreviated.

The scientific names used in this book incorporate the most recent changes in nomenclature. Readers may know some of the plants by other names.

Mojave Yucca (*Yucca schidigera*) and Joshua tree (*Yucca brevifolia*) on a rocky bajada in the northern Mojave Desert. The plants bloom again and again throughout their lives.

STEVE MULLIGAN

Ironwood (*Olneya tesota*) and saguaro (*Carnegiea gigantea*) line a shallow drainage in the Sonoran Desert. Widely spaced creosote bush (*Larrea tridentata*) thrives on the more arid flats.

JACK DYKINGA

Century plants (*Agave* sp.) dot the foreground cliffs in this Chihuahuan Desert scene. The leafy rosettes bloom once, then die.

11

Autumn in the Great Basin Desert, with rubber rabbitbrush (*Chrysothamnus nauseosus*) in fruit. This shrub has many varieties throughout the western United States.

STEVE MULLIGAN

A Sonoran Desert spring, with brittlebush (*Encelia farinosa*) and ocotillo (*Fouquieria splendens*) in full bloom. The saguaro (*Carnegiea gigantea*) will not flower for another month.

JACK DYKINGA

# Canyon ragweed

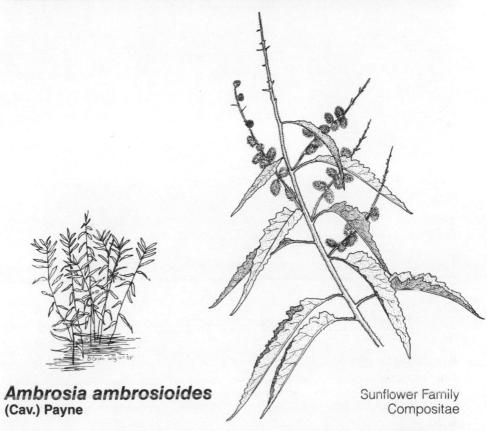

## *Ambrosia ambrosioides*
**(Cav.) Payne**

Sunflower Family
Compositae

The big, toothed leaves and cockleburlike fruits of canyon ragweed are unmistakable in washes and along roadsides throughout southern Arizona. Especially on warm, sunny days, the foliage smells noticeably rank. Because of its generous leaves and large size, canyon ragweed loses more water to the atmosphere than thriftier desert shrubs and is restricted to habitats where extra runoff is available.

In the spring, these three-foot-tall shrubs bear panicles of inconspicuous flowers at the branch tips. Many people are allergic to the pollen. Canyon ragweed belongs to the sunflower family, and every "flower" is actually a flower head containing several individual blossoms. Canyon ragweed stamens and pistils are borne in separate heads. The pistillate, or female, heads look like miniature green burs, while the staminate, or male, ones look like circular brushes. Pollen blown from plant to plant fertilizes the pistillate heads, which mature into spiny burs. Each bur is derived from three individual flowers that behave as a unit. Because their spines are hooked, the burs sometimes cling to passing animals, hitching a ride as a means of dispersal.

# Triangle-leaf bursage

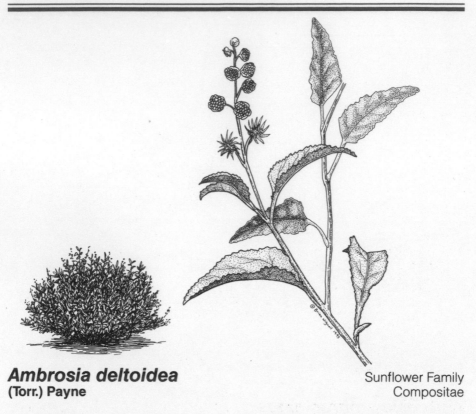

## *Ambrosia deltoidea*
**(Torr.) Payne**

Sunflower Family
Compositae

This small, unassuming plant is a linchpin of vegetation in the northern Sonoran Desert. Over many square miles of rocky or gravelly plains and hills, it is the most abundant shrub, particularly in communities of littleleaf paloverde and saguaro.

The plants look their best after winter rains have brought forth a crop of new leaves. At other times of year, especially during the hot, dry season from late April to early July, triangle-leaf bursage is little more than a collection of bare sticks. This drought-deciduous habit eliminates the need for soil moisture in months when none is available. After summer rains start, the plants make a half-hearted effort to put on new leaves, but not until winter rains return do the canopies leaf out fully.

This bursage, like its close relatives, gets its common name from the aromatic leaves and spiny fruits. Though produced in abundance, it is a rare fruit that results in a mature plant. Many of the seeds are devoured by ants and rodents soon after ripening. Many more never receive enough early autumn rain for germination to take place. When the seeds do germinate, a large number of the seedlings die of drought within a year or two. Those few seedlings that manage to become established can expect to live fifty years or more.

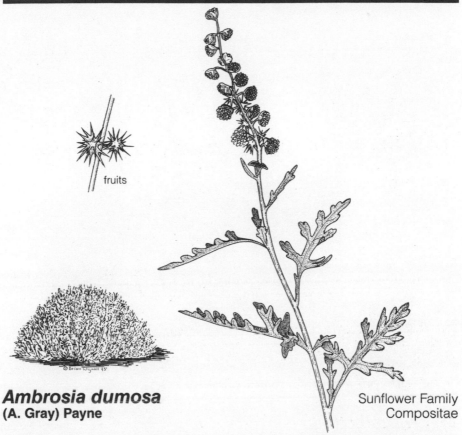

fruits

## *Ambrosia dumosa*
**(A. Gray) Payne**

Sunflower Family
Compositae

White bursage, together with creosote bush, dominates many thousands of square miles of desert in western Arizona and southeastern California. The small, sturdy shrubs, as compact as hassocks, are abundant on gravelly plains, volcanic rubble, rocky hillslopes, and even dunes. Its phenomenal success is due partly to precise adaptation to its arid environment. Thanks to their minute, fernlike divisions, the leaves lose minimal moisture to the air. When the soil becomes so dry that photosynthesis is no longer possible, the leaves wither and eventually drop off. Dense, white hairs reflect much of the incoming sunlight and keep leaf temperatures from rising too high.

If precision is one key to the success of white bursage, plasticity is another. Plants in the Mojave Desert, a winter-rainy region, produce new shoots and leaves in early spring. In the Sonoran Desert, where precipitation is biseasonal, white bursage can grow in both winter and summer, given sufficient rainfall.

The inconspicuous flowers appear early in the spring and eventually produce small, burlike fruits that can be transported in animal fur.

# Hollyleaf bursage

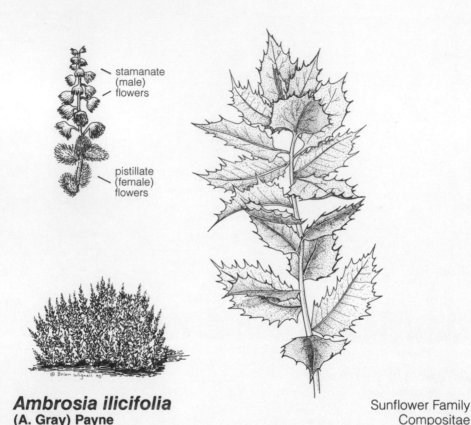

stamanate
(male)
flowers

pistillate
(female)
flowers

© Brian Wignall 93

## *Ambrosia ilicifolia*
**(A. Gray) Payne**

Sunflower Family
Compositae

The common name of this sprawling shrub echoes its scientific name, which comes from the Latin word for holly, Ilex, and means "holly-leaved." In its large leaves and cockleburlike fruits, hollyleaf bursage resembles canyon ragweed, a close relative, but its clasping leaves, edged with spiny teeth, are distinctive. The gray skeletons of dead leaves cling to the plants for a long time, possibly because plant parts decay slowly in the very arid regions where hollyleaf bursage grows.

Restricted to canyons and washes of the lower Colorado River valley and northern Baja California, this species is one of about a dozen different bursages that have evolved in the deserts of the southwestern United States and northernwestern Mexico. Each seems specialized to occupy a different portion of the climatic gradient. Hollyleaf bursage requires mild, wet winters and hot, dry summers. The rare cold snaps that can ruin the winter citrus crop in Yuma, Arizona, can also damage the leaves and stems of hollyleaf bursage.

# Big sagebrush

## *Artemisia tridentata*
**Nutt.**

Sunflower Family
Compositae

There's no smell quite like the clean and aromatic scent of big sagebrush after a rainstorm. The fragrance originates in small, oily leaf hairs, which contain chemicals called terpenoids. Like many plant chemicals, the terpenoids in big sagebrush are natural insecticides that deter caterpillars, grasshoppers and other small herbivores. The silvery color of the foliage comes from dense, T-shaped hairs. These reflect excess sunlight, keeping leaf temperatures from rising to lethal levels. They also trap air next to the leaf surface, raising humidity and lowering water loss.

Although big sagebrush grows in the so-called "cold desert" of the Great Basin, the plants still experience summer heat and long periods of little rainfall, often both at once. They cope with seasonal water stress by ceasing growth; in fact, during the late summer they lose many leaves. The remaining leaves stay on the plants all winter long, so that as soon as the soil warms up in the spring, they are ready to grow. New shoots and leaves appear in May and June, a time when the soil is still moist from winter rains and temperatures are cool.

Thirty-two thousand years ago, big sagebrush grew in the Ajo Mountains of southwestern Arizona, now a hot desert where paloverde and saguaro are the dominant plants. Ancient fragments of big sagebrush, discovered in fossilized packrat middens, suggest that the regional climate must once have much cooler and moister.

Nowadays, big sagebrush is found farther north, from northeastern Arizona and adjacent New Mexico to Oregon, Idaho, and Wyoming. In the western United States as a whole, the species dominates some ninety million acres.

# Burrobush

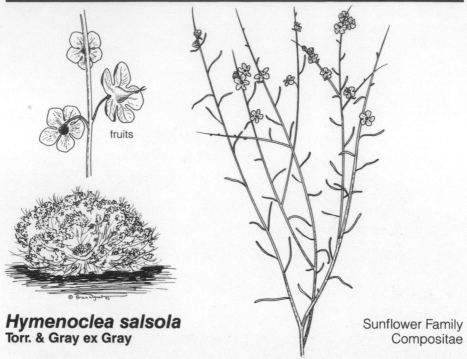

fruits

## *Hymenoclea salsola*
**Torr. & Gray ex Gray**

Sunflower Family
Compositae

The most distinctive thing about burrobush is the papery fruits. These are derived from the inconspicuous flower heads, each containing a single, minute flower inside a series of green, overlapping bracts. As the seed inside matures, the bracts lose their green color and become dry, flat wings that float the seed on the wind.

Burrobush colonizes disturbed sites such as washes, roadsides, abandoned townsites and former farm fields. Like most plants that thrive on disturbance, burrobush displays a large seed output, quick growth and short life. Carried by the wind, the seeds quickly reach newly damaged areas. The plants achieve maturity rapidly, then die about the time the land starts to heal. In the desert wash habitat, floods sometimes uproot or flatten burrobush plants, but since they can regenerate from buried stems and roots, the population quickly recovers.

Many of the younger twigs are green and capable of photosynthesis. In fact, the stems produce nearly as much sugar as the threadlike leaves, especially in the spring, when the soil is moist from winter rains. Later in the season, the shrubs lose many of their leaves as the soil dries out.

Burrobush reaches five or six feet in height and flowers in the spring. It can be found in southern California and Arizona. A similar species, also called burrobush (*Hymenoclea monogyra* Torr. & Gray ex Gray), flowers in the fall and grows from Arizona into western Texas.

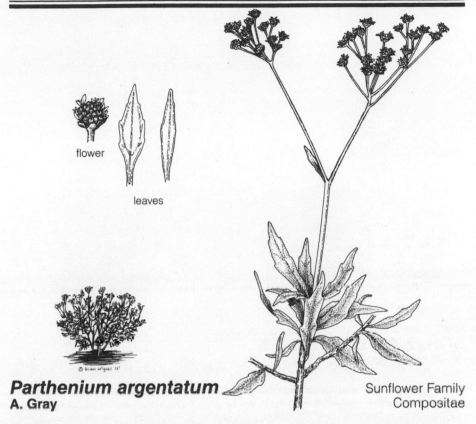

flower

leaves

## *Parthenium argentatum*
A. Gray

Sunflower Family
Compositae

Tires have been made from guayule, a two-foot-high shrub common on limestone soils in western Texas and northeastern Mexico. Many wild plants contain small amounts of rubber, but guayule is unusual in the amount and quality of the rubber it yields. Guayule rubber compares favorably with that from *Hevea brasiliensis* Willd. ex A. Juss., the Brazilian rubber tree, and can be used wherever a durable, heat-resistant rubber is needed, as in airplane tires. During World War II, when the United States could no longer obtain rubber from the Southwest Pacific, enough guayule was planted and processed to supply more than 440 tons of rubber.

Natural rubber is a good example of what scientists once considered to be unnecessary compounds, or "secondary plant chemicals." Now it is widely recognized that the so-called secondary plant chemicals, rubber among them, are vital in deterring insects and perhaps other gnawing, chewing, and sucking herbivores.

A close relative of guayule, mariola (*Parthenium incanum* H.B.K.), is scattered from Arizona to Texas, often on limestone or caliche. It, too, contains rubber and has been used commercially to a small extent.

# Pickleweed

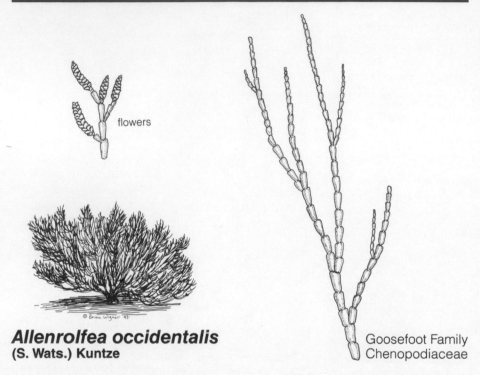

flowers

*Allenrolfea occidentalis*
**(S. Wats.) Kuntze**

Goosefoot Family
Chenopodiaceae

This aptly named shrub, which grows in rounded clumps about three feet tall and wide, does indeed resemble tiny pickles stacked end to end. The chains of pickles are actually modified stems, just as the joints of cholla or the pads of prickly pear are modified stems. Depending on moisture availability, pickleweed may be green, red, or even somewhat yellow. Pickleweed stems, like those of cholla and prickly pear, are photosynthetic: they turn water and carbon dioxide into the sugars needed for growth. Pickleweed is not a cactus, however; it has evolved stem photosynthesis independently.

Like prickly pears and chollas, pickleweeds are succulent, but for a different reason. Succulence enables cacti to survive long droughts. Atmospheric drought is seldom a problem for pickleweed, however, since the plants usually grow near playas and river bottoms where moisture lies close to the surface. On the other hand, pickleweed often contends with soil drought, a result of the salty soils typical of its preferred habitat. In plants and soils, water follows a gradient from regions of low salt to regions of high salt. When grown in salty conditions, ordinary plants quickly lose water to the soil and die. But the succulent tissues of pickleweed store salt molecules, which causes soil water to flow the other way, from the ground into the plant. Pickleweed and its associates are often called halophytes, which means "salt-lovers." It occurs from California and Nevada into Colorado and Texas.

# Seepweed

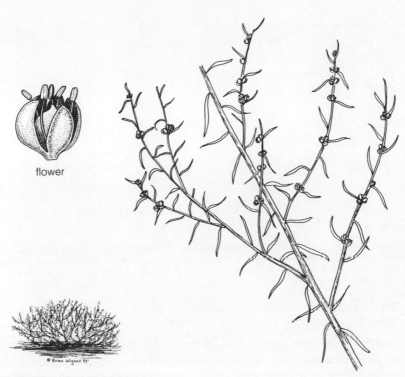

flower

## *Suaeda torreyana*
**S. Wats.**

Goosefoot Family
Chenopodiaceae

Seepweed, conspicuous mostly by its abundance, is a three-foot-tall shrub found in alkaline flats and salt marshes. The few species, like seepweed, that can tolerate such extremely saline environments tend to dominate the scene, growing in pure or nearly pure stands.

Seepweed leaves are small, flat and fleshy. Their succulence is crucial to survival in saline habitats. In plants and soils, water follows a gradient from regions of low salt to regions of high salt. Ordinary plants, grown in salty conditions, quickly lose water to the soil and die. Seepweed foils this process with its succulent tissues, which serve as storage depots for salt molecules. By creating a local region of high salt concentration, seepweed encourages water to flow from salty ground into the even saltier plant. Seepweed and its associates are often called halophytes, which means "salt-lovers."

The inconspicuous flowers eventually produce abundant hard seeds, which Native Americans have ground for pinole, a fine flour. Sometimes the young plants have been used for greens.

# Shadscale

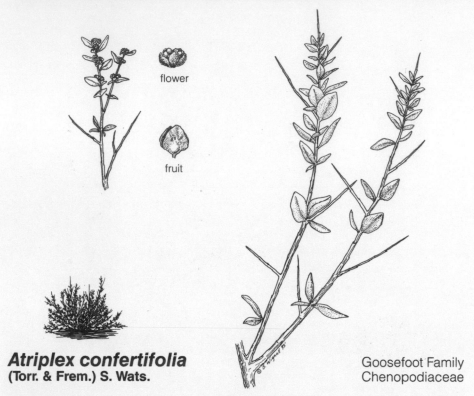

flower

fruit

## Atriplex confertifolia
**(Torr. & Frem.) S. Wats.**

Goosefoot Family
Chenopodiaceae

   Shadscale, a rounded, one- to two-foot-tall shrub, is sometimes called spiny saltbush because the old stem tips become rigid and sharply pointed. The small leaves vary in shape from nearly circular to elliptic or oblong and have smooth margins. During the winter, the plants are typically leafless. Winter rains and snows stimulate spring leafing and flowering. Shadscale fruits, thickly clustered near the branch tips, consist of a seed enclosed within two leaf-sized bracts. The bracts often turn red or pink as they mature, putting on a showier display than the inconspicuous flowers.

   Across much of Nevada and Utah, shadscale is the dominant plant for hundreds of square miles, especially on silty flats and gravelly plains. This regional dominance is partly due to shadscale's ability to thrive where other species cannot — in closed drainage basins where nighttime temperatures often drop below freezing and where the fine-textured, somewhat salty soils are stingy with moisture. Since few woody species can thrive under this combination of conditions, shadscale has little competition and can occupy most of the available space.

   Shadscale also occurs in eastern California, northern Arizona, northwestern New Mexico, and adjacent states.

# Four-wing saltbush

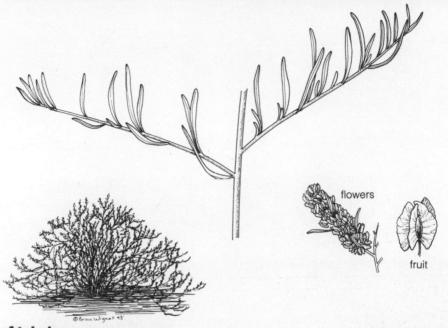

flowers

fruit

© Brian Wignall '93

## *Atriplex canescens*
**(Pursh) Nutt.**

Goosefoot Family
Chenopodiaceae

Four-wing saltbush, a stiffly-branched shrub about four or five feet tall, gets its name from the winged fruits. The wings, formed from flower bracts, are designed for wind dispersal. Each fruit contains a single seed. The inconspicuous flowers seem hardly worth a second glance. Some plants bear pistillate, or female, flowers; others carry the staminate, or male, flowers. Wind blows pollen from the staminate to the pistillate plants. The sex ratio varies somewhat from one place to another; generally it is about 60 percent female, 36 percent male, and 4 percent "undecided." Male plants require less water than females, so females are apt to switch sex during drought or in response to competition from nearby plants. Females may also switch sex after a heavy seed-bearing year. Because pollen production requires less energy than fruit production, sex-switchers can accumulate energy reserves for the following year.

A phenomenally successful species, four-wing saltbush occurs throughout the western United States from sea level to seven thousand feet and from desert to pine forest. Alkaline plains, rocky slopes, and stable dunes are a few of the many habitats where it thrives. Part of its success is due to ecotypic differentiation — the evolution of different forms to suit different habitats and climates. Plant breeders have even developed a variety that performs well on the toxic soils of mine wastes.

# Desert holly

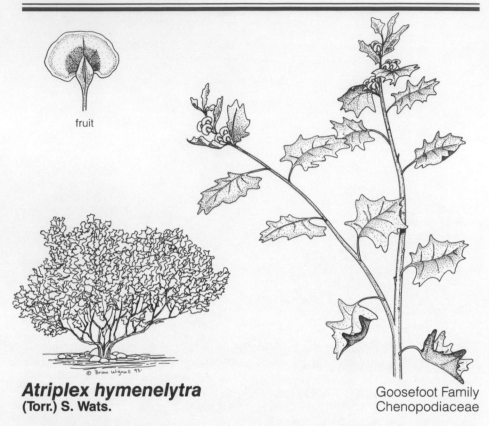

fruit

*Atriplex hymenelytra*
(Torr.) S. Wats.

Goosefoot Family
Chenopodiaceae

The jagged leaves of desert holly change color and texture with the desert's seasons, which are not the same as the calendar's. During the winter rainy season and in early spring, the leaves are pale green on the outside, succulent on the inside. By midsummer, they have turned silvery and brittle; if you didn't know better, you might think they were dead.

Desert holly thrives in the hottest, driest regions of North America where even creosote bush, that quintessential desert plant, cannot survive. Sometimes desert holly is the only woody plant in sight. Some of its adaptations to extreme deserts are external. The leaves, for instance, are nearly vertical, which means that, during most of the day, sunlight does not beat directly upon them, as it would if they were horizontal. When silvery, as in summer, they reflect much of the sunlight that does strike the surface. Minimizing the input of sunlight keeps leaf temperatures from rising to fatal levels.

Other adaptations are internal. Desert holly can withstand drought stress that would kill most plants. Even during the heat of midsummer, when many other desert plants have lost their leaves and become dormant, desert holly continues to photosynthesize, albeit at a low level.

# Desert saltbush

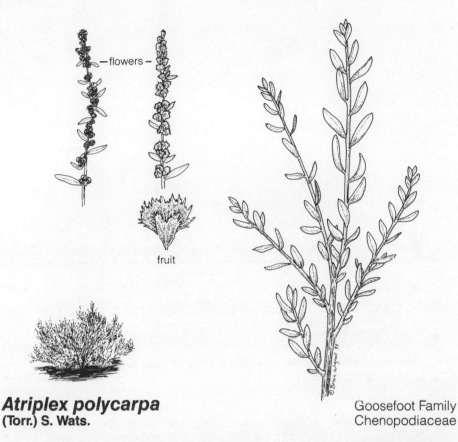

flowers

fruit

## *Atriplex polycarpa*
**(Torr.) S. Wats.**

Goosefoot Family
Chenopodiaceae

Conspicuous if only by its abundance, desert saltbush often grows in nearly pure stands on wide valleys and plains from southern California to east-central Arizona. The tiny, gray-green leaves, seldom more than one-half inch long, are often clustered in bundles.

Saltbushes often thrive in ground that is too salty for most plants, which typically lose water to the soil, then die. By accumulating salt in its tissues, desert saltbush reverses the process and draws water from the ground into the plant. As salts accumulate in the leaves, they are flushed into the bladder-like leaf hairs, which eventually burst.

Desert saltbush leaves, like those of other saltbushes, are so unusual that botanists have a special term to describe them: scurfy. To the naked eye, a scurfy leaf looks blistered or shredded. Under magnification, the blisters can be seen for what they are: exploded hairs that have discharged salt granules onto the leaf.

# Crucifixion thorn

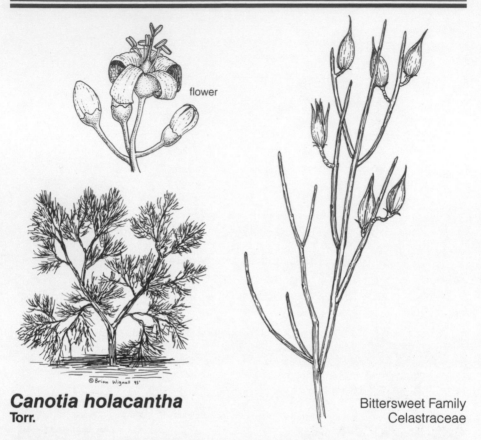

flower

*Canotia holacantha*
Torr.

Bittersweet Family
Celastraceae

This is one of several desert plants commonly known as crucifixion thorn, crown of thorns, or corona de cristo. Although all have green, leafless, thorny stems, their flowers and fruits are very different. This crucifixion thorn has small, waxy, greenish flowers and woody seed-pods shaped like goblets. In evolving to inhabit an arid environment, the various kinds of crucifixion thorn have converged upon a similar life-form. Leaflessness lowers their need for water. Green stems take the place of leaves and carry on the work of photosynthesis. Thorniness may deter browsing animals.

A bushy tree six to eighteen feet high, crucifixion thorn closely resembles foothill paloverde, especially when neither is in flower. Here again, convergent evolution has been at work. Crucifixion thorn is more frost-tolerant, and its branchlets are straight rather than zigzag. The distribution of the two species is complementary, which is not surprising. As prominent trees of slopes and plains, they fulfill a similar ecological role and would compete if they grew side by side. Often found on limestone, crucifixion thorn replaces yellow paloverde in central Arizona and along the Colorado River in Grand Canyon.

flower

## Castela emoryi
### (A. Gray) Moran & Felger

Bittersweet Family
Celastraceae

Corona de cristo is another of the green, leafless, thorny shrubs so prominent in the desert Southwest. Its most distinctive features are the stout branches and the dark brown clusters of one-seeded pods, which remain on the plants for several years. From a distance, the clusters look like birds' nests.

In corona de cristo, the stem tips become stiff and thornlike with age. Some say that thorns deter browsing animals. Others, pointing out that camels and goats eat fiercely thorny acacia trees, contend that thorniness simply happens as desert plants adjust to seasonal drought.

Juvenile corona de cristo plants are quite leafy, which enables them to quickly manufacture sugars for growth, but also increases their need for water and makes them liable to wilt or even wither during the driest months.

Corona de cristo can be found on silty plains in southwestern Arizona and adjacent southeastern California.

# Netleaf hackberry

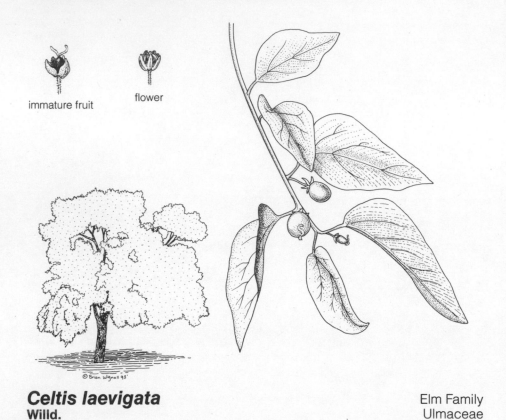

immature fruit

flower

© Brian Wignall 93

## *Celtis laevigata*
**Willd.**

Elm Family
Ulmaceae

Netleaf hackberry, a deciduous tree, is found along watercourses in the western United States and northern Mexico. Distinctive features include the strongly veiny pattern on the undersides of leaves and the orange or vermillion fruits, which taste sweet but consist mostly of seed. Small green galls often disfigure the leaves, giving them a warty appearance.

At least two species of hackberry butterflies (*Asterocampa clyton texana* and *Asterocampa celtis antonia*) rely on the foliage as caterpillar food. All summer, the adults can be found in groves of netleaf hackberry.

This plant has not always been restricted to intermittent and perennial streams. Several million years ago, the regional climate was much wetter, and many tree species now found only along major streams thrived on slopes and plains. This great deciduous forest included hackberry, cottonwood, willow, sycamore and many other sizable trees. Today, with the ascendance of an arid climate, these species have retreated to the riparian zone, where they are assured of finding enough water.

# Desert hackberry

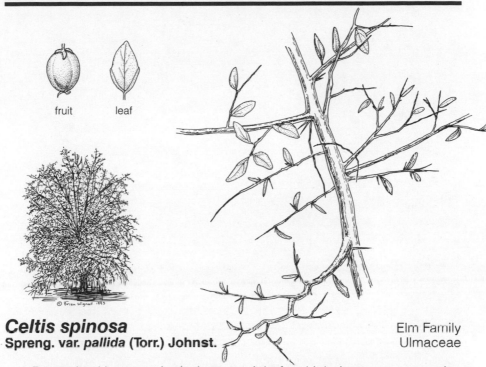

fruit    leaf

## *Celtis spinosa*
### Spreng. var. *pallida* (Torr.) Johnst.

Elm Family
Ulmaceae

Desert hackberry, a shrub three to eight feet high, is easy to recognize because of its straight, paired spines and dense, boxy habit. Hackberry leaves can vary wildly in size and shape. Generally, they are oval and not much more than a half-inch long, but the foliage of new shoots can be luxuriant, with leaves up to two inches in length. Sometimes the leaf edges are scalloped, sometimes not. Nominally evergreen, the leaves may drop in response to severe cold snaps or prolonged drought.

There are nearly a dozen Spanish common names for desert hackberry, which is not surprising since its distribution extends from the Southwest through Mexico and Central America into Argentina. In fact, over most of its range, this isn't a *desert* hackberry at all. Basically, it is a plant of the tropics and subtropics that reaches its northern limit in southern Arizona, where it grows along washes and on rocky slopes. In western Texas, desert hackberry can be abundant on floodplains and in brushy grasslands. Winter cold probably keeps the species from moving farther north.

Birds, coyotes, foxes, and javelina relish the small, orange berries, which ripen throughout the summer and fall. By feeding on the fruits, these animals help disperse the seeds. Caterpillars of hackberry and snout butterflies (*Asterocampa leilia* and *Libytheana bachmanii larvata*) eat the foliage, as do deer. The dense shrubs also provide cover for quail and nesting sites for white winged doves.

# Buckthorns

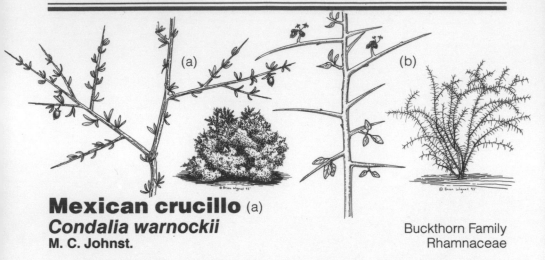

## Mexican crucillo (a)
### *Condalia warnockii*
**M. C. Johnst.**

Buckthorn Family
Rhamnaceae

This five-foot-tall shrub is so densely branched that from a distance it looks dark green or even black. Numerous tiny leaves, each no more than a quarter-inch long, contribute to its compact appearance. Despite its forbidding aspect, Mexican crucillo is actually not strongly armed; its branches are fairly flexible, and its thorns are relatively weak.

The inconspicuous flowers, borne from March to November after rains, produce succulent, blackish fruits that are notably sweet, especially compared with the acrid fruits of bitter condalia, a close relative.

## Graythorn (b)
### *Ziziphus obtusifolia*
**(Hook. ex T. & Gray) A. Gray**

Buckthorn Family
Rhamnaceae

Zigzag branches, ashy gray with velvety hairs, help distinguish the five- to eight-foot-tall graythorn from the many other thorny plants of southwestern deserts. Each of the numerous branchlets forms a right angle with the main stem and ends in a sharp, rigid point. The small leaves fall during dry periods.

Graythorn thrives in a variety of situations—silty floodplains, sandy washes, rocky slopes, and gravelly plains. This flexibility is mirrored in its wide distribution—from southeastern California and northwestern Arizona through southern New Mexico into central Texas and well south into Mexico.

The inconspicuous flowers bloom off and on throughout the year. They eventually produce succulent, dark blue fruits like miniature plums that birds relish. Native peoples no doubt have valued graythorn more as medicine than as food. The roots can be especially useful: Pima Indians have steeped them in water for bathing sore eyes, and Seri Indians have powdered them for treating skin and scalp sores.

# Sotol

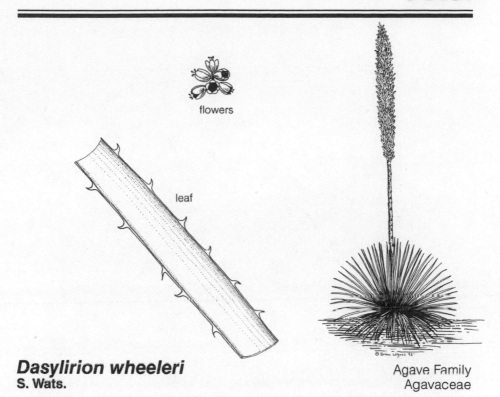

flowers

leaf

## *Dasylirion wheeleri*
**S. Wats.**

Agave Family
Agavaceae

Another common name for sotol, desert spoon, comes from the enlarged bases of the long, serrated leaves. You can easily see them in dead plants that are falling apart. Sometimes these "spoons" are used in flower arrangements. The enlarged leaf bases clasp the stem in densely overlapping spirals. This arrangement produces the rosette of leaves so characteristic of plants in the agave family.

The tall, thick flowering stalks elongate in the late spring and bloom from May to August. Male and female flowers, borne on separate plants, are wind-pollinated. Each seed is contained within a papery, three-winged shell that, upon ripening, quickly disperses in the wind.

Sotol was once a plant of many uses. Native Americans stripped the leaves of thorns, then wove them into baskets, mats and thatch. When separated from their fleshy matrix, the fibers of the youngest leaves made good rope. The immature flowering stalks could be cooked and eaten, even distilled into an alcholic beverage. In parts of Mexico, a liquor known locally as sotol is still made. It has a strong taste and leaves a raspy feeling in the throat.

The common sotol of western Texas is another species, *Dasylirion leiophyllum* Engelm. ex Trel. It differs in having the prickles on the leaf margin directed down instead of up.

# Hopbush

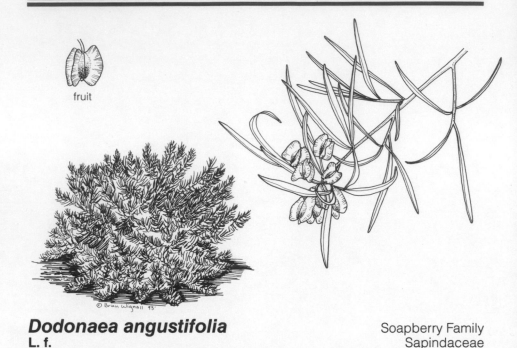

fruit

## *Dodonaea angustifolia*
L. f.

Soapberry Family
Sapindaceae

Hopbush flowers are inconspicuous, but the light, three-winged fruits, clustered at the branch tips, are not. Their resemblance to the fruits of cultivated hops gives this species its common name, but the two are not related, and hopbush cannot be used in making beer.

A farflung plant, hopbush grows wild in Colombia, Brazil, China, India, and many other places in the tropics and subtropics. Present in most Central American countries and nearly every state of Mexico, hopbush straggles north into Arizona and finally halts at the Mogollon Rim, where winters become too severe for this frost-tender species.

Part of its phenomenal success is due to its dependence upon wind for dispersal of pollen and seeds. Plants that rely on animals for these tasks don't always get good service: insect pollinators may be scarce in drought years, for instance. Wind seldom fails, and many species that rely on wind for pollination are widespread. Another reason for the success of hopbush is its preference for disturbance. Anywhere the seeds blow, they are likely to find habitats such as roadsides, old burns, and overgrazed ranges. The plants tolerate a variety of soil types, too.

Hopbush leaves are evergreen. A resinous substance makes them sticky and somewhat shiny. Underneath the resins is a waxy layer. This double coat of shellac makes the leaves resistant to water loss and no doubt deters many plant-eating insects, too.

# Mexican mormon tea

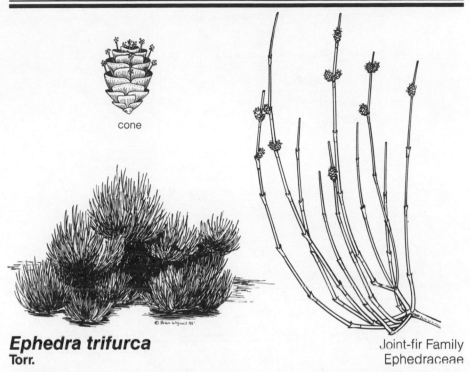

cone

## *Ephedra trifurca*
Torr.

Joint-fir Family
Ephedraceae

The mormon teas are peculiar plants of ancient lineage. Like conifers (pine, Douglas fir, and spruce, for example) they bear cones instead of fruits, but that's where the resemblance ends. Mormon tea cones are flimsy, not stiff, and the plants are desert shrubs, not forest trees. Conifers produce abundant needles, which are modified leaves; the mormon teas bear neither needles nor leaves, only thin green stems.

Mexican mormon tea, a five-foot-tall shrub, is common on gravelly plains, rocky slopes, and even stable dunes. The green stems substitute for leaves in photosynthesis. Conifers rely on wind pollination. Abundant pollen, produced in male cones, is carried by the wind to female cones on other plants. Much pollen collects on the stems beneath the anthers and is wasted. Mexican mormon tea avoids this problem to some extent by the adroit design of its cones. The scales of the male cones are placed to create turbulent air currents so that when the pollen grains spill, they are swept away from the stems.

Mexican mormon tea can be found from western Arizona into western Texas. There are several other mormon teas in the Southwest deserts; all look much like this one. Torrey mormon tea (*Ephedra torreyana* S. Wats.) occurs in western Texas. In northern Arizona, southern Nevada, and adjacent California green mormon tea (*Ephedra viridis* Cov.) and boundary mormon tea (*Ephedra nevadensis* S. Wats.) are locally common.

# Velvet ash

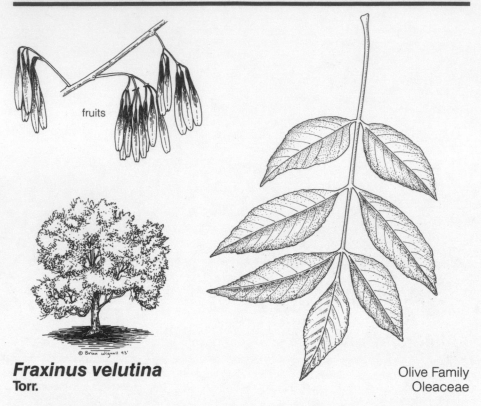

fruits

*Fraxinus velutina*
Torr.

Olive Family
Oleaceae

Velvet ash, a deciduous tree of streambeds and riverbanks, flowers early in the spring before the leaves unfold. That way, the pollen can drift from the male to the female flowers with as little interference as possible. The papery, flat fruits, which look like exclamation points, dangle in dense clusters at the stem tips until wind blows them away. Velvet ash leaves, like those of walnut, are divided into leaflets, five to nine per leaf. Walnut leaflets have toothed margins, while velvet ash leaflets are smooth.

Like other riparian trees of the desert, velvet ash is not adapted to an arid climate at all since the leaves have no mechanisms to prevent water loss. If the roots did not have access to permanent moisture, the trees would quickly die. The streamside habitat represents a final retreat for velvet ash and certain other riparian trees. Several million years ago, during the Tertiary epoch, the regional climate was substantially moister than it is now. Velvet ash, Frémont cotton-wood, netleaf hackberry, and Arizona sycamore belonged to a great decidu-ous forest that blanketed the valleys and hills. Now, forced to survive under much drier conditions, velvet ash is restricted to riversides and streambeds.

Velvet ash can be found from southern Nevada and Utah into Arizona, New Mexico, and western Texas.

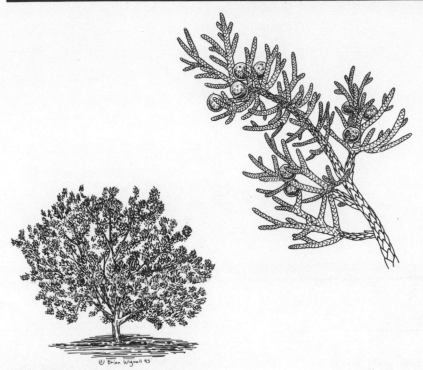

## *Juniperus monosperma*
**(Engelm.) Sarg.**

Cypress Family
Cupressaceae

One-seed juniper, a shrubby tree with shreddy bark, looks out of place among desert plants like sotol and saguaro. In a way, the species is out of place in the small mountain ranges where desertscrub is continuous from the bottom to the top. In these arid ranges, one-seed juniper is a relic of the cooler and wetter Pleistocene era, when woodlands of pinyon and juniper thrived where desert plants eke out a meager living now. The trees we see today are not ten thousand years old, of course; they are the modern remnants of former forests.

In the desert mountain ranges of western Arizona, one-seed juniper tends to grow in the shade of cliffs and on north-facing slopes, relatively moist habitats where seasonal aridity is somewhat ameliorated. Elsewhere in the Southwest, it grows on rocky hills and mesas, generally at the lower edge of woodland.

The soft, bluish berries are actually cones, since juniper is a conifer, like pine or spruce. Birds relish the cones and no doubt disperse the seeds from place to place. The wood makes a fragrant campfire that burns quite hot. It has been used for fenceposts and corrals.

# Pallid wolfberry

fruit

## *Lycium pallidum*
**Miers**

Nightshade Family
Solanaceae

This is the most distinctive wolfberry in the desert Southwest. The leaves, much larger than on any other wolfberry, are bluish-white and waxy, and the greenish flowers are nearly an inch long. Like all wolfberries, this one is thorny. It is unusual, however, in that its leaves are evergreen, or nearly so, instead of drought-deciduous.

Pallid wolfberry fruits prolifically in the late spring and summer. The succulent, red berries of this particular species are somewhat bitter, but Native Americans could seldom afford to ignore such an abundant resource. They ate the berries fresh and also dried them for later use. (A few species with much sweeter berries also bear abundant fruits, and these were eaten as well.) Birds and other animals feed avidly upon the berries and no doubt disperse the seeds from place to place.

Because the leaves remain on the plants year-round, pallid wolfberry has a higher demand for water than its drought-deciduous relatives. In the desert, it tends to grow in washes where runoff supplements natural rainfall. At higher elevations, pallid wolfberry can be found on rocky slopes and plains. It grows from southern California to Texas and in the adjacent states of Utah and Colorado.

# Beargrass

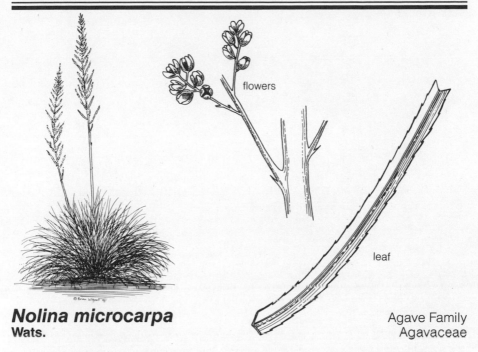

flowers

leaf

## *Nolina microcarpa*
**Wats.**

Agave Family
Agavaceae

Although commonly called beargrass, this plant is not a grass at all. It is a member of the Agave Family, and among its relatives are the yuccas, agaves, and sotols. Finely toothed along the margins, beargrass leaves can inflict painful cuts on unwary fingers. The leaf bases clasp the stem in densely overlapping spirals, an arrangement that produces the rosette of leaves so characteristic of the Agave Family.

Beargrass rosettes make dense, fountainlike clumps on hillsides and canyon slopes at the upper margin of the desert. Each rosette arises from a creeping stem that is partly buried in the soil. Wildfires consume the leaves and char the aboveground portion of the stem; but, since the growing point is protected underground, new leaves soon appear from the old, burned growth.

In May and June, flowering stalks push their way above the leaves. The inconspicuous flowers are most likely wind-pollinated; nevertheless, they produce enough nectar or pollen to attract a multitude of bees and wasps. Long after the small, round seeds have dispersed, the flowering stalks remain in place like ragged bottle brushes.

The fibrous leaves have long been used in basketry by Native Americans. In northern Mexico, they are still collected for making brooms. Beargrass grows from Arizona to Texas. A similar species, *Nolina texana* S. Wats., can be found in southeastern Arizona and western Texas. *Nolina bigelovii* (Torr.) S. Wats. of western Arizona and southern California has a definite trunk and wide leaves.

# Teddy bear cholla

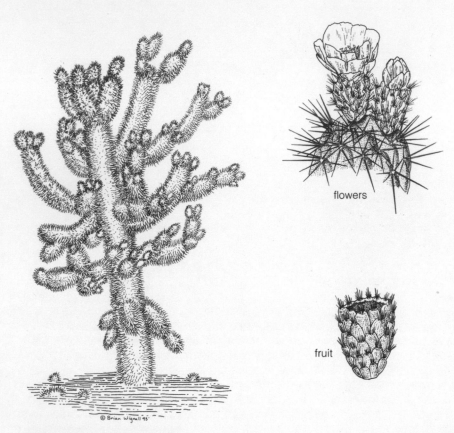

flowers

fruit

© Brian Wignall 93

## *Opuntia bigelovii*
**Engelm.**

Cactus Family
Cactaceae

When people or their pets tangle with the spiny joints of teddy bear cholla, the encounter is usually a painful one. The barbed spines pierce tender skin easily and are extracted only with difficulty. It is all the more amazing, therefore, that desert packrats can handle cholla joints with impunity. They build their characteristic dens by mounding cholla joints with other detritus, such as sticks and prickly pear pads, and they clear tiny pathways through otherwise impenetrable cholla thickets, making a quick and safe retreat from coyotes, foxes, and other predators.

Teddy bear cholla, a thicket-forming plant of rocky slopes and plains, can be found in the warmer parts of southeastern California, southern Arizona, and adjacent Mexico.

# Arizona sycamore

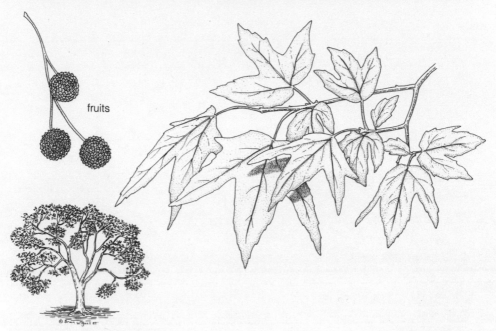

fruits

## Platanus wrightii
**S. Wats.**

Sycamore Family
Platanaceae

The arching branches, five-fingered leaves, and smooth, white bark of Arizona sycamore are a familiar sight along desert and woodland watercourses in Arizona and New Mexico. These huge trees require ample moisture and are never found far from water. They often tap underground streams. Several million years ago, when the regional climate was milder and wetter than it is now, Arizona sycamore and other riparian trees blanketed hillslopes in a vast deciduous forest. As the climate became more arid, these forest trees retreated to canyon bottoms and streamsides, the only habitats where they could find enough moisture.

The seeds are borne in dense ball-like clusters. Although the trees are fairly prolific — a mature sycamore produces thousands of seeds each year — sycamore seedlings are not very common in the wild, mostly because germination requirements are met infrequently. The short-lived seeds ripen from October to May and germinate only when the soil is warm and wet. In most years, they die before summer rains bring about the right combination of warmth and moisture. Even in years when the seeds do germinate, the seedlings are vulnerable to withering from drought, scouring in flash floods, and trampling by cattle. Fortunately, the trees are long-lived and often reproduce vegetatively by sending up suckers from the root crown.

# Frémont cottonwood

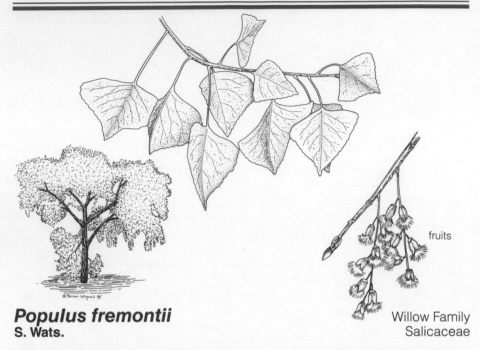

fruits

*Populus fremontii*
S. Wats.

Willow Family
Salicaceae

Although this big, riparian tree was named for its wood, which is light and tough but not particularly durable, the name applies equally well to the seeds, which are tufted with cottony hairs. The wind-borne seeds typically disperse as receding spring floodwaters expose moist reaches of sand, which are ideal for seed germination. Since cottonwood seeds lose viability after only five weeks, the timing of spring floods is crucial. Seedlings quickly develop long roots that tap moist sand well below the surface. Thus, as the upper layers of sand dry out, the seedlings are able to survive.

In the Mexican state of Sonora, young cottonwoods are used as living wiers. Farmers attach fresh, young cottonwood branches to barbed wire fences that follow or cross streams. The cuttings quickly root in the moist sand; soon, they put out new, leafy shoots, as well. This living fence traps the nutrient-rich sediment of floodwaters, making a rich medium for agriculture.

Frémont cottonwood thrives wherever there is abundant surface or sub-surface water. The wide, flat-topped canopies are a familiar and much-loved sight along the streams and rivers from California to western Texas. These gallery forests are typically rich in bird and animal life, especially in comparison to the surrounding agricultural land.

This tree was named in honor of John C. Frémont, explorer, presidential candidate, and territorial governor of Arizona. Although primarily a politician, Frémont routinely collected plants during his travels throughout the American West. Several of the new species he found bear his name in commemoration.

# Goodding willow

## Salix gooddingii
Ball

Willow Family
Salicaceae

In its best form, Goodding willow is a graceful tree thirty or forty feet tall with arching branches and trailing foliage. Sometimes it is a much shrubbier plant, reaching only ten or twelve feet. In either case, the yellowish twigs and finely toothed, lance-shaped leaves help distinguish this willow from others. Like all willows, Goodding willow loves moist areas and is found only near permanent water, which may lie above or below the surface.

The seeds of Goodding willow are shed in late May and early June when streambed surfaces are dry and hot. Flooding from summer rains moistens the sand, giving the seeds of willows and other riparian trees a chance to germinate. But, since Goodding willow seeds lose their viability in only nine or ten weeks, the entire seed crop can fail if summer rains are late or spotty. Even in years when the seeds do germinate, the seedlings face other hazards: browsing and trampling by cattle, scouring in flash floods and desiccation in drought.

*Salix gooddingii* was named to honor Leslie Goodding, a botanist with the Soil Conservation Service from 1918 to 1944. He collected plants throughout the western United States and pushed for conservation of Sycamore Canyon in Santa Cruz County, Arizona. A portion of the canyon known for its rich flora and natural beauty has been designated the Goodding Research Natural Area.

# Jojoba

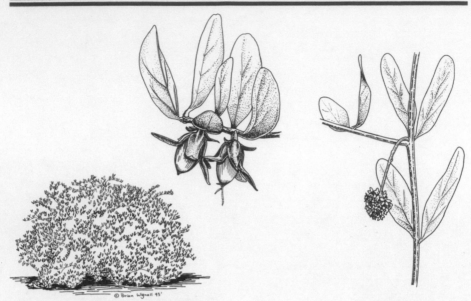

## Simmondsia chinensis
**(Link) Schneid.**

Jojoba Family
Simmondsiaceae

The Spanish common name for this desert shrub is pronounced ho-HO-ba. With its dense canopy of evergreen leaves, jojoba may seem unfit for survival in the desert, but is extremely drought resistant. The leaves contain a high percentage of dry matter, which makes them rigid and therefore resistant to wilting. All are oriented vertically, so they intercept sunlight only early in the morning and late in the afternoon. By restricting photosynthesis to the relatively cool hours of the day, the plants conserve water.

Because they contain a compound related to cyanide, jojoba seeds, eaten in large quantity, are toxic to mammals, with the exception of the Bailey's pocket mouse, which has evolved a detoxification mechanism that renders the seeds harmless. In collecting and storing the seeds, Bailey's pocket mice act as jojoba gardeners, since the seeds that aren't eaten may germinate eventually, often as dense clusters of seedlings.

Ground jojoba seeds have long been used by Indians for shampoo and medicine. These days, the seed oil (actually a liquid wax) is considered a valuable substitute for oil from the endangered sperm whale. A variety of shampoos, cosmetics, soaps, lubricants, and pharmaceuticals contain jojoba oil. The demand is great enough that jojoba plantations have sprung up in western Arizona and southeastern California, typically in broad, silty valleys where planting and harvesting can be readily mechanized. In the wild, jojoba grows on rocky canyon slopes and along gravelly washes in southern California and Arizona.

## *Vitis arizonica*
**Engelm.**

Grape Family
Vitaceae

This scrambling or sprawling vine is sometimes called canyon grape because it grows in well-watered canyons from southern Nevada and Utah through Arizona and New Mexico into western Texas. Like the riparian trees with which it often grows — sycamore, velvet ash, cottonwood, willow — Arizona grape is hardly a desert plant. It requires deep and thorough irrigation and is never found far from permanent water.

The tendrils are weak; even so, the twining, woody stems often clamber into the upper branches of large trees. Arizona grape sometimes kills shrubs and small trees by shading them so thoroughly that their leaves cannot catch the sun to photosynthesize.

Appearing from April to June, the inconspicuous flowers are extraordinarily sweet-scented and attract large numbers of bees and other insects. The tasty, blackish-blue berries, which ripen by autumn, make excellent jelly and juice. Birds usually manage to strip the vines of fruit well before would-be jelly makers arrive.

A close relative, desert grape (*Vitis girardiana* Munson), grows in canyons at the edge of the Mojave Desert in southern California. It has cobwebby leaves and long, branched tendrils.

# Desert fan palm

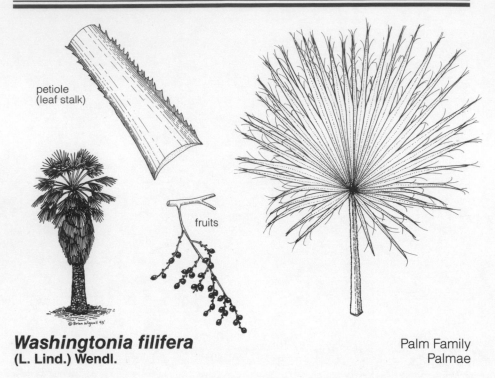

petiole
(leaf stalk)

fruits

## *Washingtonia filifera*
**(L. Lind.) Wendl.**

Palm Family
Palmae

Although many kinds of palms are cultivated in the desert cities of Arizona and California, this is the only palm native to the southwestern United States. Fossils show that ten million years ago the species extended from the Mojave Desert to the Pacific Coast. Geologic and climatic changes eliminated it from much of this area, and today it is found in the low deserts of western Arizona and southeastern California, typically in steep side canyons near small, trickling streams.

The frond of a desert fan palm—actually a single leaf—may reach six feet or more in width. The characteristic accordion pleats give the leaf rigidity, preventing it from collapsing like a flag on a still day. If undisturbed, the leaves accumulate around the trunk as they die, eventually making a shaggy skirt some forty or fifty feet long. Too often, however, vandals burn the skirts, producing naked, blackened trunks.

Native Americans once found many uses for the desert fan palm: they thatched their dwellings with its leaves, wove the leaf fibers into ropes and baskets, preserved the fruits, and ground the seeds into meal. They may well have planted seeds in appropriate locations, thus multiplying the number of groves. Birds and coyotes eat the fruits, which are wrinkled and dry but nutritious. The seeds pass unharmed through the coyote digestive tract, and, as a result, coyotes disperse the species.

# Catclaw

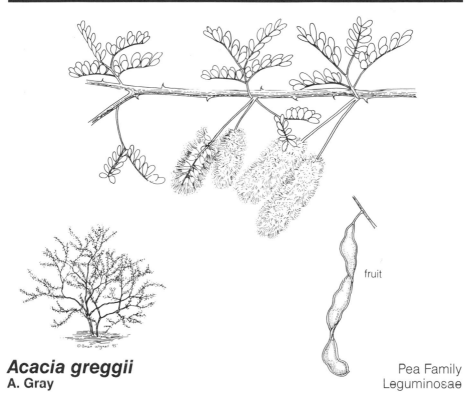

fruit

## *Acacia greggii*
**A. Gray**

Pea Family
Leguminosae

Children sometimes call this the "Frito" plant because the wide, flat fruits are often twisted or curled like corn chips. The two halves of the fruit separate to reveal dark seeds shaped like oversize lentils. Like the seeds of many legumes, those of catclaw won't germinate until they have been scarified. You can do this yourself by nicking the seeds with a razor blade. Nature does it by tumbling them in the floodwaters of sandy washes.

The creamy flowers, which cluster together in caterpillar-like spikes, appear in April and May. They are sweet-scented and attract a wide variety of bees, hoverflies, wasps, and butterflies. Ants get into the act, too: they visit the sugar-exuding nectary on the leaf axis. Honeybees make excellent honey from catclaw nectar.

Catclaw is more tolerant of cold weather than most acacias and occurs as far north as southern Nevada and southwestern Utah. Where winters are mild, as in the Mexican states of Sonora and Chihuahua, catclaw can be a tree up to twenty feet tall. Over much of its northern range, however, it is a spreading shrub not much more than five or six feet in height. Catclaw is found most often along sandy washes. It can live to be a hundred years or older. The distinctive spines, shaped like a cat's claw, give this species its common name.

# Samota

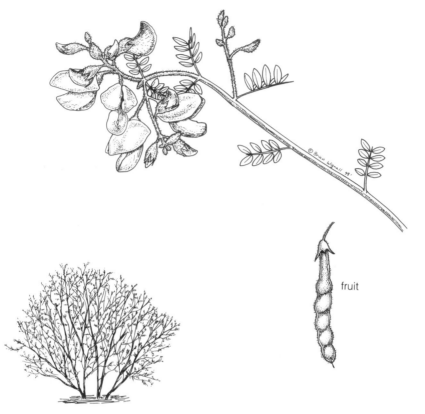

fruit

## *Coursetia glandulosa*
A. Gray

Pea Family
Leguminosae

When samota starts to bloom in February and March, the stems are often bare. The pretty little pea flowers are white and yellow, tinged with lavender or red. Small native bees are the main pollinators. Leaves appear shortly after the flowers, and by April, the plants are fully leafed out. Samota loses its leaves with the first hard frost in the fall.

Samota grows on rocky canyon slopes and in sandy washes in southern Arizona. The five- to fifteen-foot-tall shrubs are locally common. Although this species looks like a desert plant, its distribution extends far south into Central America, and it is best regarded as a tropical thornscrub species that manages to survive in arid environments. The branch tips are easily damaged by low temperatures. Winter cold probably keeps the species from moving farther north.

# Wait-a-minute bush

flowers

© Brian Wignall 43

## *Mimosa biuncifera*
**Benth.**

Pea Family
Leguminosae

This shrub urges passersby to "wait a minute" by sinking its cat-claw spines into clothing or flesh. Even the leaves and pods are prickly with tiny, curved spines. Because the stem spines are curved and paired (two at every node), wait-a-minute bush is easy to distinguish from catclaw (which has one curved spine per node) and white thorn (which has paired, straight spines).

The individual flowers are not much longer than an eyelash, but when massed in fragrant, cream-colored balls, they make a showy display that attracts bees, wasps, beeflies, and butterflies. Only a few flowers in each inflorescence produce fruits; the rest eventually fall unfertilized. Since they help attract pollinators and dispense pollen, however, they are not wasted.

Wait-a-minute leaves are divided into tiny leaflets, as many as three hundred per leaf. New leaves appear rather late in the spring and are retained all summer. They turn brown with the first frosts and drop soon afterward. Flowers are borne between May and August. Even without flowers and leaves, the five-foot-tall shrubs are readily recognized by their paired, catclaw spines and tendency to grow in impenetrable thickets. Wait-a-minute thrives on hillslopes and in washes from Arizona to Texas.

# Honey mesquite

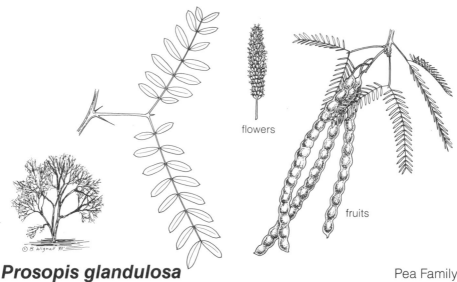

flowers

fruits

## *Prosopis glandulosa*
### Torr. var. *torreyana* (L. Benson) M. C. Johnst.

Pea Family
Leguminosae

   Until recent times, the native peoples of the Southwest hardly could have survived without the mesquite. Most tribes have used every part of the plant, from the sugar-rich pods to the fibrous roots.

   The ripening of the seed pods just before the summer rains turned the harshest season into a time of plenty. Some tribes have different names for the pods at various stages of ripening. Traditionally, the pods have been gathered when dry, then toasted. The toasted pods have been pounded, seeds and all, into a fine-textured flour. After winnowing to remove the seeds, a second grinding reduces the seeds to powder. Both kinds of flour have been baked into rolls and cakes.

   The hard, water-resistant wood not only has provided fuel and building materials, it also has been fashioned into many useful objects — bowls, balls, planting sticks, awls, war clubs, trays, pestles, cradles and more. The roots, after being separated into fibers, have been twisted into cordage. The leaves, steeped as a tea, have been used for treating sore eyes and stomach disorders. Even the black pitch that oozes out of the trunks has been used as medicinal tea, hair dye, and pottery paint.

   Modern-day Southwesterners have a love-hate relationship with the mesquite. City dwellers love the flavor that mesquite charcoal gives their steaks and chops, while ranchers seek to eradicate the trees from formerly grassy rangelands. Honey mesquite can be found from western Texas and Oklahoma to southern California, and south into Mexico. It ranges in size from spreading, five-foot-tall shrubs to graceful, thirty-foot-tall trees. The creamy or yellowish flowers, borne in dense, cylindrical spikes, appear in late spring.

# Screwbean mesquite

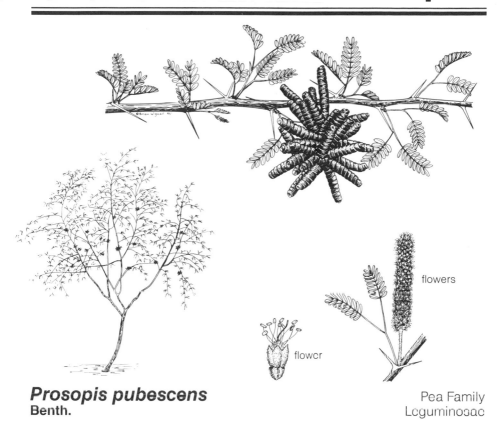

flowers

flower

## *Prosopis pubescens*
**Benth.**

Pea Family
Leguminosae

Its distinctive pods make this mesquite easy to recognize. They are tightly coiled, like springs, and the coils are compressed together. The function of spiraled pods is not known. Perhaps coiling used to prevent attack by the tiny, black bruchid beetles that hollow out the seeds of mesquites and other legumes. If so, bruchid beetles have since figured out the system, because their holes are just as evident on screwbean pods as on those of velvet and honey mesquite.

There are other possibilities, too. Unlike most leguminous pods, which split to scatter their seeds, those of the various mesquites remain sealed. Eventually cattle eat the pods and distribute the seeds, neatly packaged in clumps of fertilizer, about the landscape. Before cattle came along, mammals like giant ground sloths and native horses, now extinct in North America, no doubt ate and dispersed mesquite seeds. The coiled pods of screwbean mesquite may reflect some interaction with these long-gone dispersal agents.

Screwbean mesquite, a small tree ten to fifteen feet tall, generally grows in moist places as near waterholes and along streams. The creamy or yellowish flowers, crowded together in long spikes, appear in May.

# Velvet mesquite

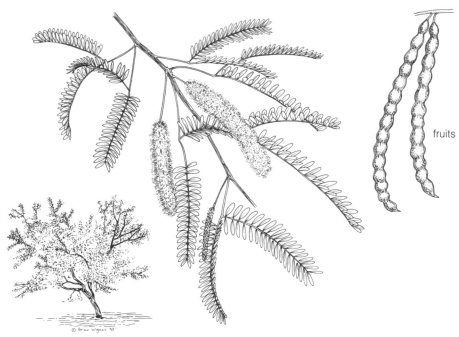

fruits

## *Prosopis velutina*
**Woot.**

Pea Family
Leguminosae

A single flower of velvet mesquite is only a few millimeters long. When clustered together in long, creamy spikes, however, the flowers make a showy display that attracts an incredible variety of pollinators, including sixty species of native bees. Wasps, beetles, flies, and introduced honeybees also visit the blossoms in April, May, and June. Only a few of the flowers in each inflorescence produce fruits. The rest, which eventually fall unfertilized, are not wasted, however; they contribute to the showy display that attracts pollinators.

Each year, a mature mesquite tree can produce more than thirty-five pounds of fruit, about 140,000 seeds altogether, and it produces them regardless of heat, drought, or cold. Only in years of extreme frost does the crop of mesquite beans fail. Reliable production of mesquite beans depends on abundant resources of food (from the leafy canopy) and water (from underground supplies). Even if every flower were fertilized, the tree would not have enough resources to turn them all into ripened seeds.

A thirty-foot-tall tree with brown, shreddy bark, velvet mesquite closely resembles honey mesquite, and they can be difficult to tell apart. In general, velvet mesquite leaflets are appropriately velvety to the touch, whereas those of honey mesquite are hairless or nearly so. Velvet mesquite is found in Arizona, westernmost New Mexico, and in the Mexican state of Sonora.

# Oreganillo

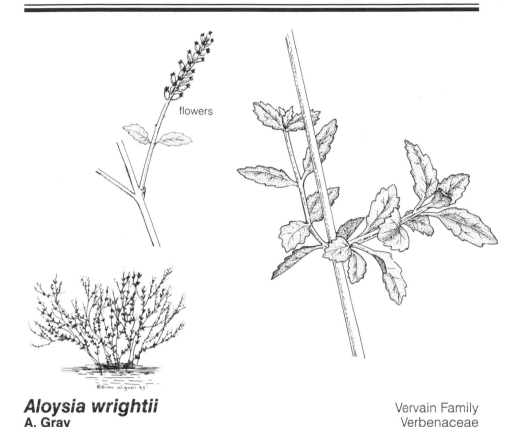

flowers

## *Aloysia wrightii*
**A. Gray**

Vervain Family
Verbenaceae

The small leaves of this four- to five-foot-tall shrub are scalloped and embossed with a waffle pattern. When crushed or rubbed, they smell something like oregano, thus the Spanish common name "oreganillo." Beekeepers sometimes call this species "bee brush" because honeybees love the mildly sweet, white flowers. Like many desert shrubs, oreganillo blooms in spring and again in summer if rains have been adequate. The leaves wither and drop during dry periods; new leaves appear after rain has moistened the soil again.

Oreganillo is often quite common on rocky slopes and along canyon streambeds from southeastern California into West Texas. At low elevations, oreganillo grows on rocky, north-facing slopes, which are relatively cool and moist. At somewhat higher elevations, winter cold is more of a consideration than summer drought, and the shrubs can be found on warm, dry, south-facing slopes.

Many desert shrubs, oreganillo among them, seem to change size hardly at all once they reach maturity. Slow growth in woody plants is often associated with long life: oreganillo may live seventy-five years or more.

# Wax milkweed

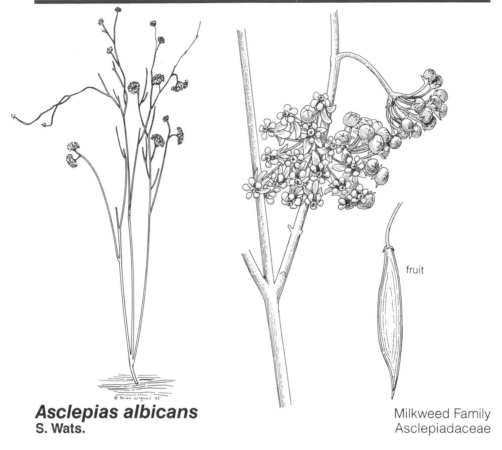

© Brian Wignall '93

## *Asclepias albicans*
**S. Wats.**

Milkweed Family
Asclepiadaceae

fruit

Easterners familiar with leafy milkweeds of pastures and roadsides might be startled by this bare-bones version, found on rocky slopes in the more arid portions of the Sonoran Desert. The long, gangly stems, which lack leaves and may reach six feet or more in height, are thickly coated with flakes of white wax. The flowers, however, look much the same as milkweed flowers every-where, as do the familiar pods bursting with white fluff and brown seeds.

In spring you might see queen butterflies fluttering over wax milkweed stems, or you might find their multicolored caterpillars feeding among the flowers. Queens, like monarchs, lay their eggs only on milkweeds, which con-tain noxious chemicals; by consuming milkweed leaves and flowers, the lar-vae become poisonous themselves and are avoided by birds and perhaps other predators.

When broken, the stems exude the copious milky latex of their kind. The latex contains natural rubber, up to five percent of the plant's dry weight. No commercial use of this rubber has been made.

# Desert milkweed

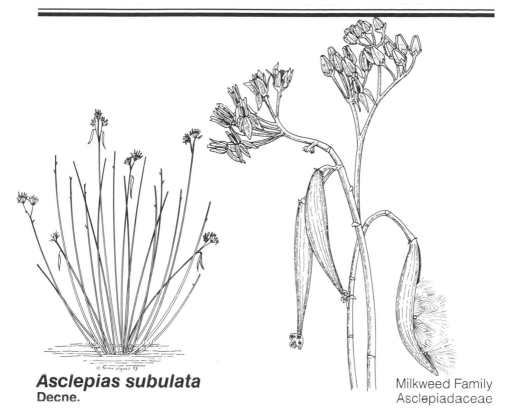

**_Asclepias subulata_**
Decne.

Milkweed Family
Asclepiadaceae

When desert milkweed blooms in the spring, you can sometimes hear the plants before you see them, so dense is the population of buzzing insect visitors. A variety of wasps, bees, and hoverflies gather to sip nectar from the flowers, and you are almost assured of seeing a tarantula hawk—a large, orange-bodied wasp with blue-black wings—among them. Although the larvae of these giant wasps feed on tarantulas that the female wasp has captured and paralyzed, the adult wasps feed on flower nectar.

The milkweed flower, an extraordinarily complicated structure, is composed of an inner circle of nectar sacks, called hoods, and an outer circle of triangular petals, all folded downward. Milkweed pollen is prepackaged in pollinia, which resemble tiny wishbones and are tucked between the hoods. Pollinia are highly specialized to clip onto the legs of an insect visitor, then unclip when inserted into another milkweed flower. Large insects, like the tarantula hawk, make the best milkweed pollinators. Smaller insects are just as apt to leave a leg behind as to take a pollinium away.

The clumped, rushlike plants are three to four feet tall and can be found at roadsides and in other disturbed spots in the lower Colorado River valley and the adjacent, low-lying desert.

# Seep willow

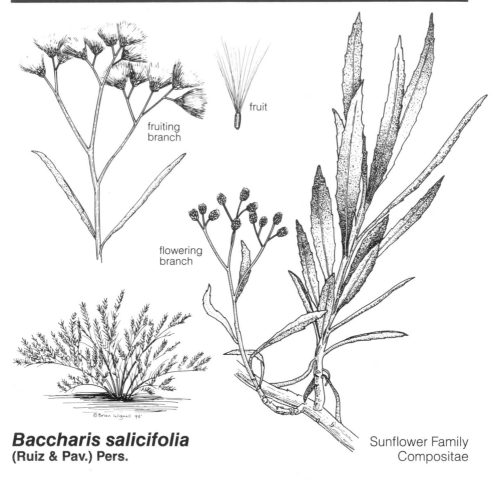

fruiting branch

fruit

flowering branch

*Baccharis salicifolia*
(Ruiz & Pav.) Pers.

Sunflower Family
Compositae

Many people might not notice when seep willow blooms, but the inconspicuous flowers do not escape the attention of insects. From spring to fall, the plants are abuzz with bees and wasps and aflutter with an astounding variety of butterflies.

Growing as far south as Guatemala and Honduras, this species is accustomed to tropical temperatures and does not mind the desert's heat as long as its roots have access to water. The six-foot-tall shrubs form graceful thickets along rivers, streambanks, and irrigation canals from southern California into southernmost Texas. Even intermittent streams provide suitable habitat as long as water is available beneath the surface. Despite its long, narrow leaves and riparian habitat, "seep willow" is not a willow at all. Instead, as its dandelion-like seeds and composite flower heads demonstrate, it is a member of the large and diverse Sunflower Family.

# Desert broom

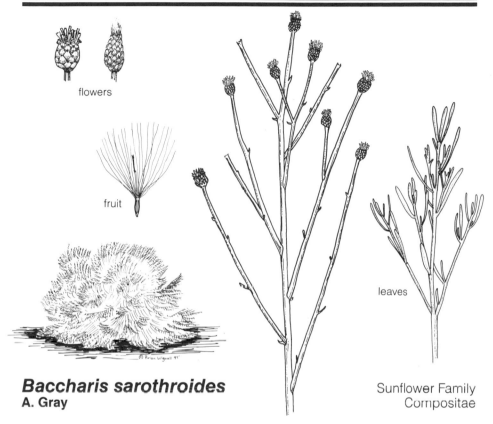

flowers

fruit

leaves

## *Baccharis sarothroides*
A. Gray

Sunflower Family
Compositae

This five-foot-tall shrub can be so abundant along highways that, when the cottony seeds disperse in late November, the desert seems adrift in snow. Desert broom prefers disturbed habitats: highway shoulders, borrow pits, gravel piles, abandoned roads, sandy washes and old burns. Like most plants that thrive on disturbance, desert broom displays a large seed output, fast growth, and short life. Its wind-borne seeds are well-suited to colonize bare areas soon after the natural vegetation has been striped away. The plants quickly grow to maturity, then die after ten to twenty years, about the time the disturbance starts to heal.

Many species have adapted to desert heat and aridity by reducing the size of their leaves. Desert broom has dispensed with leaves altogether. Since the green stems contain chlorophyll, the photosynthetic pigment usually located in leaves, they can produce the sugars necessary for growth. Leaflessness keeps water loss to a minimum and gives desert broom a jump on the competition. As soon as rain moistens the soil, desert broom can start photosythesizing; its drought-deciduous neighbors, meanwhile, are delayed by the need to produce a new crop of leaves before they can take advantage of rain.

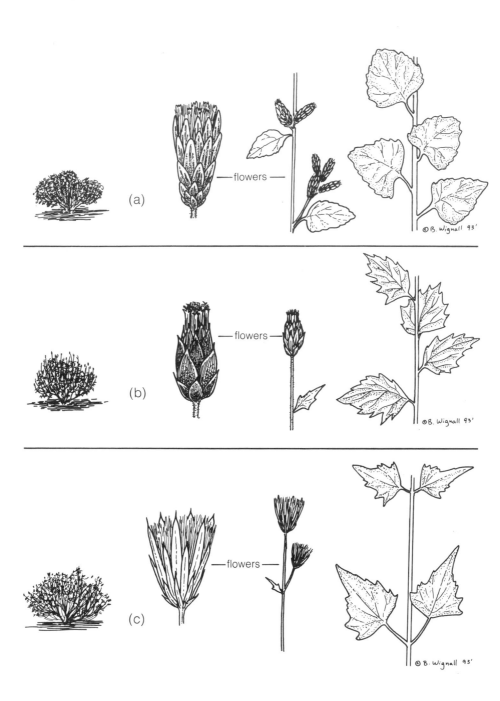

(a)    flowers

(b)    flowers

(c)    flowers

© B. Wignall 93'

© B. Wignall 93'

© B. Wignall 93'

## California brickell bush (a)
*Brickellia californica*                     Sunflower Family
(Torr. & Gray) A. Gray                       Compositae

In the Southwest, there are more than three dozen species of brickell bush, some woody, some not. All share certain characteristics. There are never any ray flowers in the thimblelike flower heads. The flowers are never yellow. Leaves of various brickell bushes are often more distinctive than their flowers.

About fourteen of the southwestern brickell bushes are truly desert species. Most are limited in distribution. When plotted on a map, the ranges of the various desert species fit together almost as neatly as the pieces of a jigsaw puzzle. Only a few are widespread, California brickell bush among them. A bushy shrub to three feet tall and wide, it occurs from California to western Texas, and as far north as Idaho and northern Colorado.

California brickell bush occurs on rocky slopes and along washes. It can be recognized by its broad, triangular, scalloped leaves and full, bushy habit.

## Holly brickell bush (b)
*Brickellia atractyloides*                   Sunflower Family
A. Gray                                       Compositae

If you spend much time hiking in the desert canyons of western Arizona, you are apt to run across holly brickell bush, a small, rounded shrub about a foot tall. The glossy, bright green leaves are embossed above and below with a network of prominent veins. In the winter, when the leaves turn gray or white, the veiny network stands out even more. The creamy flowers, clustered in tight heads about the size of a thimble, appear from March to May.

Holly brickell bush thrives on rocky slopes and in cracks in boulders. The plants may live to be quite old, a hundred years or more.

## Coulter brickell bush (c)
*Brickellia coulteri*                        Sunflower Family
A. Gray                                       Compositae

In southern Arizona, this brittle-stemmed shrub tends to grow in the shade of trees like paloverde and mesquite, where it seldom reaches more than a foot or two in height. The leaves, often tinged with purple, are inch-long triangles with several ragged teeth. In the spring, the slender flower heads appear singly at the stem tips. The wind-borne seeds disperse in May and June.

Coulter brickell bush grows from central Mexico into southern Arizona, where it reaches its northern limit. Winter cold probably keeps it from traveling farther north.

**59**

# Desert zinnia

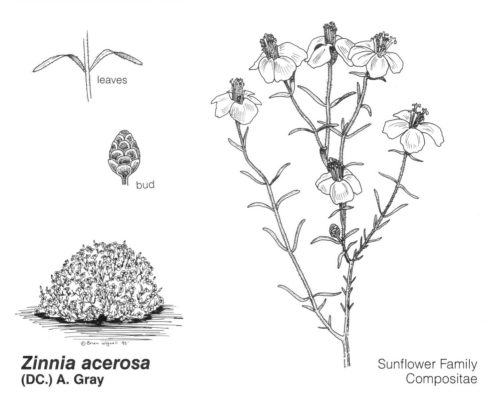

leaves

bud

© Brian Wignall 93'

## *Zinnia acerosa*
**(DC.) A. Gray**

Sunflower Family
Compositae

Desert zinnia grows no more than shin-high, but it qualifies as a shrub because the stems are woody and persistent. Found from Texas to southern Arizona and south into northern Mexico, desert zinnia often grows with creosote bush on gravelly plains. In Texas, this little sub-shrub can be abundant on soils derived from limestone. Farther west, where limestone is less common, it frequents soils rich in caliche, a limey material that sometimes forms a hard-pan in desert soils. Desert zinnia also colonizes disturbed ground, such road shoulders, abandoned dirt roads, and vacant lots.

What looks like a single flower is actually a flower head composed of several yellow disk flowers surrounded by four or five white ray flowers. This arrangement is typical of the sunflower family, which is also called the composite family after the composite flower head. By reducing the number of ray flowers, desert zinnia manages to look less like a composite and more like a regular flower. Perhaps this kind of mimicry helps it attract pollinators.

The miniscule leaves are borne in pairs on the stem. This, along with the distinctive, white-rayed flower heads, makes desert zinnia easy to recognize. Given sufficient rain, the plants flower in spring and again in summer, sometimes covering themselves with small white blossoms.

# Elephant tree

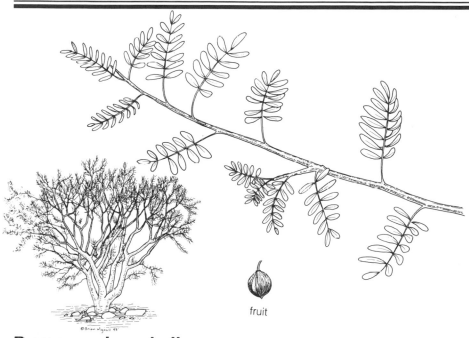

fruit

## *Bursera microphylla*
**A. Gray**

Torchwood Family
Burseraceae

When crushed, the glossy, dark green leaves of elephant tree smell like camphor. Each leaf is divided into a dozen or so small leaflets. This is a tree of contradictions: although the creamy bark of the trunk peels off in thin sheets, the cherry-red bark of the twigs clings as tight as skin; and while the trunk and main branches are swollen and rigid, the stem tips are slender and flexible.

There's a botanical term for the elephant tree life-form; it is "sarcocaulescent," which means "fleshy stem." Actually, the stems are not so much fleshy as they are moist. The wood contains 60 to 70 percent water — not as much as a saguaro but far more than a pine. Sarcocaulescence, one of many possible adaptations to an arid climate, acts as a buffer against drought, providing a source of moisture even when the soil is dry.

In the Mexican states of Sonora and Baja California, where winters are mild, elephant tree truly is a tree to twenty-five feet in height. Where the winters are colder, as in southern Arizona and southeastern California, frost frequently prunes the top branches, ensuring that elephant tree seldom grows more than five or six feet tall. When winter temperatures fall to twenty-one degrees F or lower, the shrubs are killed to the ground. Winter cold probably prevents the species from moving any farther north than its present limit, the Harquahala Mountains of western Arizona and the South Mountains near Phoenix.

# Saguaro

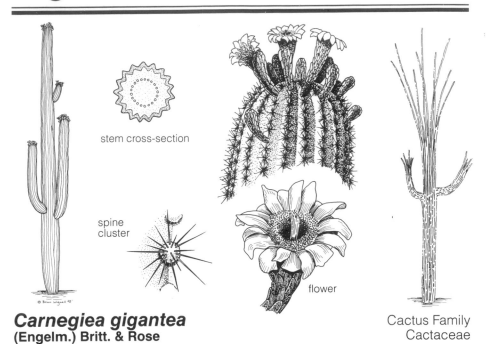

stem cross-section

spine cluster

flower

## Carnegiea gigantea
**(Engelm.) Britt. & Rose**

Cactus Family
Cactaceae

We usually do not think of cacti as trees, but what else can you call a plant that grows up to fifty feet high, weighs as much as nine tons and lives for as long as two hundred years? Saguaros start to branch when they reach fourteen to sixteen feet in height, or about seventy-five years in age. The oldest specimens may have a dozen or more branches. The interior of the saguaro is very different from that of ordinary trees. Instead of solid wood, it contains about two dozen wooden rods. This structure allows the plant to expand and contract as it gains and loses moisture.

Saguaro roots radiate up to fifty feet from the trunk. Lying close to the soil surface, they are well-placed to capture even the lightest of rainfalls. Such shallow roots sometimes prove a liability, however, as when the ground is wet from heavy rains. Then strong winds easily topple the giant plants.

Saguaro branches and trunks provide homes for wildlife. Gila woodpeckers and gilded flickers carve nesting holes in the upper branches. Later on, other birds such as elf owls, screech owls, purple martins, and house finches occupy the holes. The saguaro forms callus tissue around wounds, such as woodpecker holes. After the plants fall and decay, the hardened "boots" persist for several years.

About fifty kinds of tree-form cacti are found in deserts and thorn-forests from Argentina to Arizona. The saguaro is endemic to the Sonoran Desert and grows from southern Arizona into the Mexican state of Sonora. A few scattered populations also occur near the lower Colorado River in California.

# Desert Christmas cactus

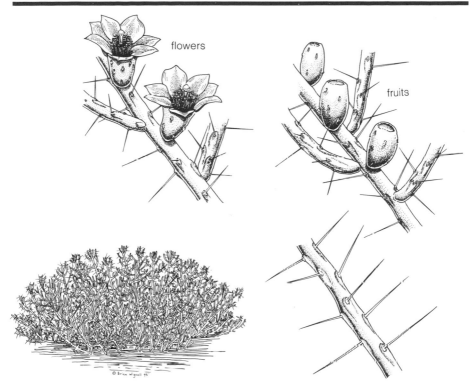

flowers

fruits

## *Opuntia leptocaulis*
**DC.**

Cactus Family
Cactaceae

Desert Christmas cactus is easy to recognize because of its slender, sprawling stems and red, berrylike fruits. The creamy flowers are small for a cactus — about the size of a quarter. They appear at the hottest time of year, in May and June, and open in the afternoon. Ripening slowly during the summer, the bright red berries still cling to the plants at Christmas-time, a conspicuous element of color in the otherwise drab winter scene. Native peoples have harvested the fruits and eaten them fresh. Although the berries lack spines, they are abundantly supplied with the tiny barbs known as glochids. Sometimes the fruits are spread on the ground and brushed with creosote bush branches to remove the barbs.

The stems of desert Christmas cactus often interlock, forming bewildering thickets that are easier to enter than to exit. Sometimes the plants climb well into the canopies of palo verde or mesquite trees. Brittle and apt to break off at the slightest touch, the fallen joints readily take root and grow into new plants. Desert Christmas cactus can be found from Arizona to Texas and in the adjacent Mexican states of Sonora and Chihuahua.

# Western virgin's bower

fruit

## *Clematis ligusticifolia*
**Nutt.**

Buttercup Family
Ranunculaceae

This is a sturdy, woody vine that clambers over trees and fences through-out much of the western United States. Each seed is tipped with a long, feath-ery plume that eventually becomes airborne. Although western virgin's bower is not adapted to the desert, it survives there anyway by growing mainly in washes where extra water is available, or in dense shade, where evaporation is lessened.

Vines climb in a variety of ways. Some modify various plant parts (a branch-let or a leaf axis, for example) into claws or tendrils. Others climb by winding their stems around any convenient object. Western virgin's bower does this, and it also employs the leaf stalk as a climbing device.

A similar species, Drummond virgin's bower (*Clematis drummondii* Torr. & Gray), also thrives in the desert Southwest. It has grayer foliage and longer plumes on the seeds than western virgin's bower.

# Cliff rose

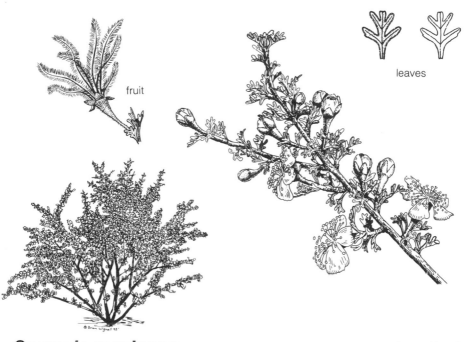

fruit

leaves

## *Cowania mexicana*
**D. Don**

Rose Family
Rosaceae

The foliage of this five- to ten-foot tall shrub is impregnated with resinous compounds that give it a bitter taste and acrid odor. Despite these chemicals, deer browse the leaves and twigs, especially in the winter when little else is available. Caterpillars of the Fotis hairstreak (*Incisalia fotis*), a small, dark brown butterfly, consume nothing but cliff rose leaves. Like many unpleasant-tasting plants, cliff rose has a number of medicinal uses, thus its other common name of quinine bush.

Cliff rose blooms from April to September, generally in response to rain. The large white flowers are sweetly fragrant and attract a variety of insect visitors, including honeybees, metallic green sweat bees, and bee flies. As insects collect pollen from the many stamens in the center of the flower, they accidentally brush against the pistils, thus transferring pollen from flower to flower. Each fertilized pistil eventually produces a single-seeded fruit called an achene. Each achene has a long, fuzzy tail, a plume that catches in the wind and disperses the seed. A single flower may produce as many as ten plumed achenes.

Cliff rose is found on rocky slopes from southeastern California through Nevada, Utah, and Arizona into western New Mexico and southwestern Colorado.

# Apache plume

***Fallugia paradoxa***
**(Don) Endl.**

Rose Family
Rosaceae

© Brian Wignall 93

Whether in flower or in fruit, Apache plume catches the eye. The five-petaled flowers are rather large, often more than an inch in diameter. After good winter rains, they blanket the plants with white. The numerous pistils in the center of the blossoms ripen into clusters of delicate plumes that look like feather dusters or sea anemones. Derived from a single pistil, each plume consists of a seed topped by the persistent style. Fine, silky hairs on the style make the plumes buoyant enough to disperse in the wind.

Apache plume can be found in desert, grassland, and woodland in Arizona, New Mexico, and adjacent portions of neighboring states. At higher elevations, the five-foot-tall shrubs thrive on plains and rocky slopes. Lower down, they generally cling to washes and roadsides, habitats where extra run-off compensates for the paucity of rainfall.

At first glance, Apache plume looks much like cliff rose, another shrub with shreddy bark, white flowers and plumed seeds. They aren't too difficult to tell apart, however. Apache plume is a spreading shrub; cliff rose more often takes the form of a small tree. Apache plume flowers are larger (about an inch across instead of half an inch) and paper-white rather than creamy in color. Each Apache plume flower produces many pinkish plumes, whereas each cliff rose flower produces about ten tawny ones.

# Desert almond

flower

## *Prunus fasciculata*
A. Gray

Rose Family
Rosaceae

Desert almond is related to the cultivated almond, but the two originated on opposite sides of the globe. Like many of our fruit and nut trees, the cultivated almond came from Central Asia. Desert almond is a local product, endemic to the Mojave Desert of southeastern California, southern Nevada, and northwestern Arizona. An intricately branched shrub three to six feet tall, it grows on rocky hillsides and plains, sometimes in thickets. The small, white flowers eventually produce half-inch-long, velvety fruits enclosing a single, large seed.

Desert almond seeds, and probably all parts of the plant, contain hydrocyanic acid, a compound related to cyanide. This same toxin also occurs in certain other members of the Rose Family—in peach seeds, for instance, which is why mothers warn their children not to crack the pits. The ancestors of our cultivated almond were no doubt poisonous, too. Domestication involved the elimination of hydrocyanic acid from the seeds, perhaps through selection of those plants that possessed the less bitter seeds.

# Arizona rosewood

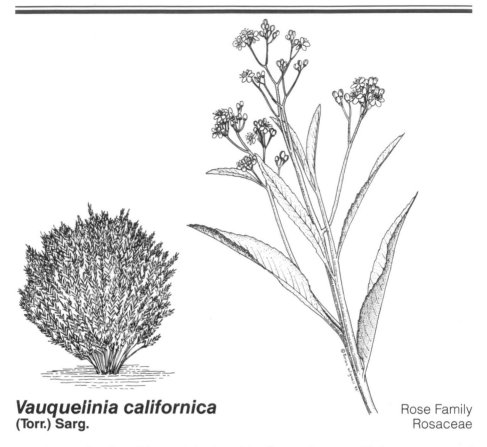

### *Vauquelinia californica*
**(Torr.) Sarg.**

Rose Family
Rosaceae

Appearing from May to July, the white flower clusters of Arizona rosewood are reminiscent of its cultivated relatives, shrubs like pyracantha and spiraea. Most people find their musky odor somewhat unpleasant. Flies like it, however, and pollinate the blossoms. Even without flowers, Arizona rosewood is a handsome shrub with its olive green, leathery leaves and reddish-brown, scaly bark. The plants grow to twenty-five feet tall and often have a boxy shape, as if recently pruned.

Arizona rosewood thrives in canyons and on mountain slopes in the transition zone between desert scrub and oak woodland. Evidently true desert is too dry for the species, and true woodland is too cold. A map of its present-day distribution shows Arizona rosewood scattered on isolated mountain ranges in southeastern Arizona — from the Superstition Mountains in the north to the Whetstone Mountains in the south. These disconnected populations are probably remnants of what was once a much wider distribution. During the last Ice Age, when the regional climate was cooler and wetter, Arizona rosewood might well have grown with oaks in the valleys between the mountains.

# Desert mock-orange

fruits

## Crossosoma bigelovii
**S. Wats.**

Crossosoma Family
Crossosomataceae

Desert mock-orange is a harbinger of spring in the mountain canyons of southeastern California and southern Arizona. The white flowers first appear in February. Their sweet and spicy fragrance is somewhat reminiscent of citrus blossoms.

The seed capsules — more properly called follicles — develop in the center of the blossoms. Each follicle contains several seeds, and each seed is wrapped in a fleshy, fringed appendange called an aril. This aril is the source of the genus name *Crossosoma*, which means "fringed body." When rich in oils, arillate seeds are often collected by ants, which remove and consume the aril and discard the seed. Perhaps the arillate seeds of desert mock-orange are dispersed by ants.

Seldom more than three or four feet tall, desert mock-orange often grows from cracks in cliffs and along washes.

# Dune buckwheat

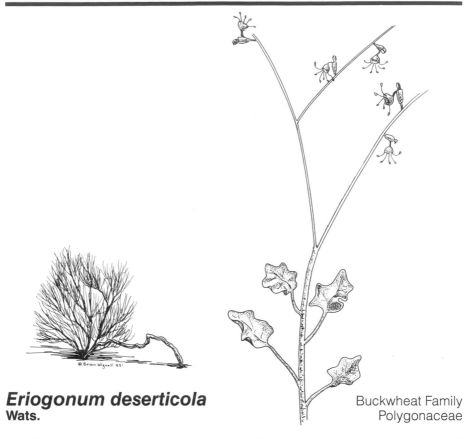

*Eriogonum deserticola*
Wats.

Buckwheat Family
Polygonaceae

Dune buckwheat, a sand dune specialist, takes on the absurd postures of a contortionist at times. Because wind-blown sand threatens to engulf everything in its path, sand dune plants must be able to grow rapidly and, like a sprig of ivy placed in water, produce adventitious roots. Rapid growth keeps leaves and flowers above the advancing dune, and adventitious roots provide support and seek out water in the shifting substrate. As dune buckwheat grows upward through an advancing dune, its stem can reach incredible lengths — twenty feet or more. Then, as the dune moves on, the stem collapses bit by bit until it resembles a length of rope or a strand of baling wire cast upon the sand. Sometimes the excavated stems look like oversized croquet wickets.

Dune buckwheat occurs in only a few places. The species is limited to active dunes in the southeastern corner of California and adjoining portions of Arizona, Sonora, and Baja California. Its narrow range is partly a consequence of extreme specialization: plants adapted to grow on dunes are poorly suited to other habitats. Moreover, in a region where dunes are rare, plants that grow only on dunes will necessarily be limited in their distribution.

# Wild buckwheat

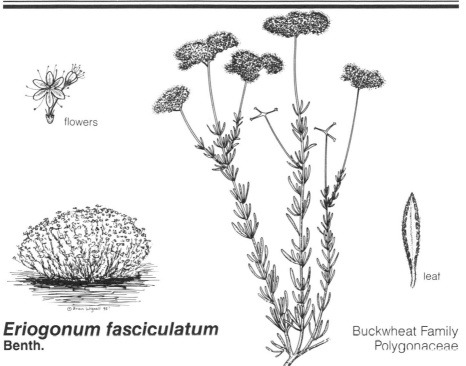

flowers

leaf

*Eriogonum fasciculatum*
**Benth.**

Buckwheat Family
Polygonaceae

This three-foot-tall shrub is especially handsome in bloom. The lacy clusters of tiny white flowers, borne on long, leafless flower stalks, are reminiscent of yarrow (*Achillea millefolium* L.) or Queen Anne's lace (*Daucus carota* L.), but the three are not related. They resemble one another because they share the same kind of inflorescence, in which small flowers are arranged in flat-topped bunches. This arrangement facilitates pollination by small, nectar-feeding insects. By offering only a tiny amount of nectar in each individual blossom, the plant encourages insects — often hoverflies and bees — to seek out other, nearby blossoms. In crawling, scrambling, and flying from one flat flower cluster to another, insects distribute the pollen.

Wild buckwheat blooms more or less continuously from March until June. Even after the flowers have died, the rust-colored inflorescences are conspicuous for several months. By virtue of their small size, leathery texture, and in-rolled margins, the evergreen leaves resist drought and frost.

This species thrives on rocky slopes from southern Nevada into southern Arizona, and is abundant in the chaparral and coastal sage scrub of southern California. In southwestern Arizona, wild buckwheat is spottily distributed. These scattered populations are remnants of what was once a continuous distribution. When the regional climate began to dry out about eight thousand years ago, wild buckwheat survived in the relatively moist environment of mountain canyons, where it is found today.

# Heartleaf limberbush

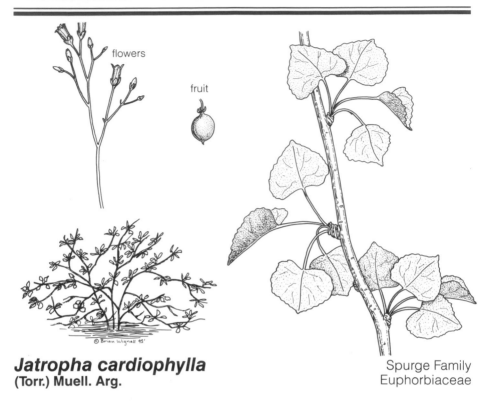

flowers

fruit

© Brian Wignall 95'

## *Jatropha cardiophylla*
**(Torr.) Muell. Arg.**

Spurge Family
Euphorbiaceae

"Sangre" is the Spanish word for blood, and this three-foot-tall shrub is known in Mexico as sangre de cristo or sangre de drago—Christ's blood or dragon's blood. The name comes from the sap, which is clear when fresh but reddish brown after it coagulates. In Arizona, the plant is generally called limberbush after the remarkably flexible stems. Bare much of the year, these put forth small, heart-shaped leaves in the hot, dry month of June. Once the summer rains start in July, the leaves double or triple in size. If the summer is dry, they remain small. Early in September they turn yellow, and, by the end of the month they are gone. Borne throughout the summer, the white flowers are bell-shaped and diminutive. The seed capsules are surprisingly large, about the size of a filbert. When the seeds are ripe, the capsule explodes, flinging its contents far and wide.

Heartleaf limberbush cannot withstand much frost. The plants often grow among rocks, which absorb heat during sunny winter days and reradiate it at night when air temperatures plummet. The stems of unprotected plants may freeze to the ground in the coldest winters. This sensitivity to cold keeps heartleaf limberbush from growing much taller than three or four feet in southern Arizona, but farther south, in the Mexican state of Sonora, the plants can become small trees.

# Wedgeleaf limberbush

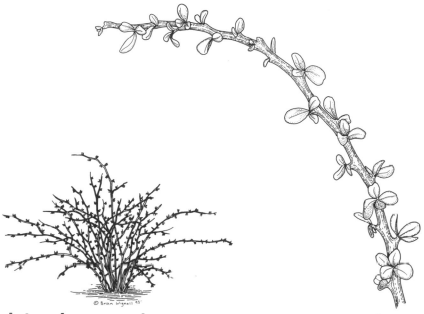

## *Jatropha cuneata*
**Wigg. & Roll.**

Spurge Family
Euphorbiaceae

Wedgeleaf limberbush is named for its wedge-shaped leaves and extra-ordinarily flexible stems. When broken, stems and leaves alike exude a clear sap that makes indelible brown stains on clothing. Clustered in bunches along the stout stems, the leaves appear with the summer rains and last until the following spring when the soil dries out. Tiny, white flowers also appear in response to summer rains.

As well as being flexible, the stems are somewhat succulent. One term for them is "sarcocaulescent," which means fleshy-stemmed. Like cacti, sar-cocaulescent plants store water in their stem tissues. This helps tide them over droughts and enables them to live in the most arid region of North America.

Although widespread along both sides of the Gulf of California, wedgeleaf limberbush has a limited distribution in Arizona. Since the plants are frost-sensitive, they grow only in the warmest desert areas, and their requirement for summer rainfall limits them still further. Wedgeleaf limberbush is often abundant where it does occur and can be the dominant plant on gravelly plains and rocky slopes.

Wedgeleaf limberbush sap has been used to treat skin eruptions, dysentery, and sore throats, and to staunch bleeding from slight wounds. Seri Indians have employed the stems in basketry and made reddish-brown dye from the roots.

# Candelilla

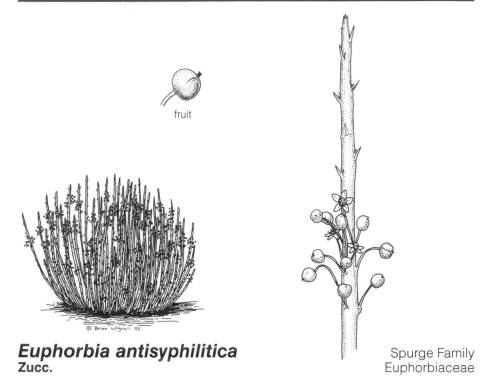

fruit

**_Euphorbia antisyphilitica_**
**Zucc.**

Spurge Family
Euphorbiaceae

The pencil-thin stems of candelilla are gray from a thick coat of wax; if you scratch them, you can see the green tissue underneath. Most of the time the plants are leafless, a water-saving adaptation to their arid environment.

Candelilla, which means "little candle," could refer equally well to the appearance of the plants or to their use. The stem wax has long been collected for making candles, soaps, shoe polish, ointments and other products. Even today, travelers in the Mexican state of Coahuila can see men and women gathering great bundles of candelilla stems, which they transport to their wax camps by burro. Stems are tossed into vats of water and boiled over wood fires. The addition of sulphuric acid peels the wax off the stems. As wax floats to the surface, it is skimmed off, set aside and eventually sold.

The plants themselves have other uses for their wax. It makes an impervious coat that helps prevent water loss and, by reflecting solar radiation, keeps stem temperatures from rising to lethal levels.

Candelilla's dainty, pink and white flowers, clustered near the stem tips, can be found from spring through fall. The clumps can be abundant on gravelly flats and limestone hills in parts of western Texas and adjacent Mexican states. Unfortunately, because the wax-makers uproot entire plants, candelilla is rapidly disappearing over much of its former range.

# Desert cotton

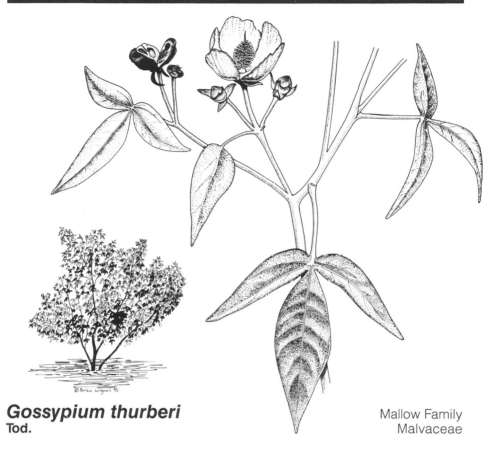

**_Gossypium thurberi_**
**Tod.**

Mallow Family
Malvaceae

Though closely related, desert cotton and cultivated cotton do not look much alike. Cultivated cotton has big, yellow flowers, while desert cotton has modest, white ones. Moreover, cultivated cotton is grown as an annual, whereas desert cotton, a woody plant, lives for several years. The biggest difference, however, lies in the seeds. Those of cultivated cotton are enveloped in thick fluff, while those of desert cotton bear only a few scraggly hairs.

Sometimes, instead of seeds, the small woody capsules contain the grubs of a certain cotton boll weevil. Although this particular weevil generally feeds only on wild cottons, it sometimes spreads to cultivated plants, and at one time the U. S. Department of Agriculture tried to eradicate desert cotton wherever it grew near cotton fields.

The cup-shaped flowers appear in the summer. Often there is a faint crimson spot at the base of each petal. Desert cotton grows on canyon slopes at the upper margin of the desert and the lower margin of oak woodland from southern Arizona into northern Mexico.

# All thorn

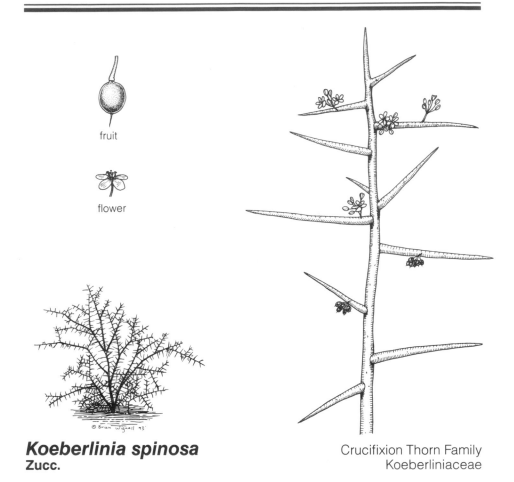

fruit

flower

**Koeberlinia spinosa**
Zucc.

Crucifixion Thorn Family
Koeberliniaceae

This well-named shrub is a mass of thorns. The rigid branches fork at right angles, and every branch, even the shortest, ends in a sharp thorn. Cattle avoid all thorn, and on overgrazed ranges the plants sometime forms impenetrable thickets.

The leafless branches of all thorn are dark green, an indication that they contain chlorophyll and can manufacture the sugars needed for growth. This, too, is typical of some desert plants. Leaflessness can be an advantage in a dry climate, since it drastically reduces water loss. On the other hand, by eliminating so much potential photosynthetic surface area, a leafless plant is constrained to grow rather slowly.

One variety of all thorn grows on plains and mesas from southeastern Arizona to western Texas. Another, often found on canyon slopes and along washes, occurs in southwestern Arizona and adjacent California.

# Berlandier wolfberry

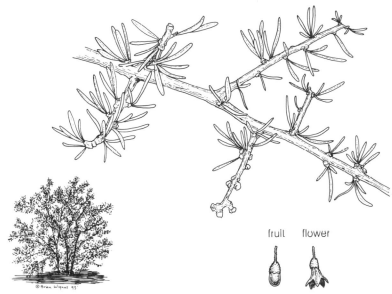

fruit    flower

## *Lycium berlandieri*
**Dunal**

Nightshade Family
Solanaceae

The dozen species of wolfberry in the desert Southwest look more or less alike. Berlandier wolfberry, a thorny shrub about four feet tall with mahogany-colored or pale gray bark, grows on rocky slopes from southern Arizona to western Texas. The bright green leaves, generally less than an inch long, are clustered in bunches. Like the leaves of many desert shrubs, they sprout and drop in response to rain and drought. The plants can survive in a leafless condition for many months.

The tiny white flowers appear at almost any time of year after plentiful rains. They smell like honey and attract honeybees and butterflies in abundance. Berlandier wolfberry is heterostylous: some bear "thrum" flowers with long stamens and short styles, while others have "pin" flowers with short stamens and long styles. The long stamens of the thrum flowers deposit pollen on one part of a bee's body; then, when the long styles of the pin flowers touch the bee at the same point, they become pollinated. The same thing happens with the short stamens of the pin flowers and the short styles of the thrum flowers. Heterostyly promotes cross-pollination, which is more beneficial to the species in the long run than self-pollination.

The small, sweet, red berries are avidly sought by birds and perhaps other animals. But, because wolfberry blooms sporadically, the fruits are an unpredictable resource. Even prolific flowering does not guarantee a good fruit crop, since the plants may flower when pollinators are scarce or when frost causes many fruits to abort.

# Mortonia

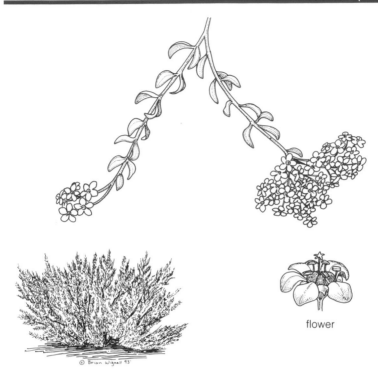

flower

## *Mortonia scabrella*
**A. Gray**

Bittersweet Family
Celastraceae

Mortonia leaves feel like coarse sandpaper. If you look at them under magnification, you can see the stout, stiff hairs that make the leaves so rough. Other distinctive characteristics are the way the leaves curl under around the edges and overlap densely along the stem.

Botanists have a term for stiff, leathery leaves like these. It is "sclerophyllous," which means "hard-leaved." Generally, it is the shrubs and trees of chaparral that are sclerophyllous. Desert plants typically possess soft, pliable leaves that simply fall off when the soil dries out or when winter temperatures plummet. In chaparral, where moisture is less erratic than in desert, shrubs tend to keep their leaves year-round. This means that the leaves must be adapted to endure cold winters and dry summers, a combination best achieved by a hard, leathery texture. The small white flowers, clustered at the branch tips, bloom from March to September. They are avidly sought by bees, wasps, butterflies, and beetles.

Mortonia reach three to five feet in height and can be common on rocky slopes and plains in western Texas. The species reaches its western limit on limestone in southeastern Arizona.

# Sandpaper plant

## *Petalonyx thurberi*
**A. Gray**

Loasa Family
Loasaceae

Sandpaper plant belongs to a family in which many members possess stinging hairs on the leaves and stems. In sandpaper plant, this potential has been diverted. The stiff, sharp, downturned hairs on its leaves and stems are so dense and so rough they feel like coarse sandpaper to the touch. Because the hairs are barbed, broken stems and leaves adhere to clothing and skin. This harshly scabrous pubescence may deter gnawing and chewing insects. By making an impenetrable barrier, the dense hairs may also keep ants from crawling up the stems to steal nectar from the flowers.

A sprawling shrub seldom more than two feet tall, sandpaper plant grows in sandy washes in southern California and southern Arizona. Its white flowers are small but pretty. Solitary bees visit the flowers and are probably the only pollinators.

# Desert sumac

## *Rhus microphylla*
**Engelm.**

Cashew Family
Anacardiaceae

Desert sumac, a broad shrub four or five feet in height, often grows as wide as it is tall. Inconspicuous white flowers are borne at the stem tips in April and May when the branches are leafless. The small, glossy leaves, divided into tiny, rounded leaflets, appear in late spring and last until the first hard frost. More noticeable than the flowers are the bright red, succulent fruits, which can be found throughout the late spring and summer.

A characteristic plant of the Chihuahuan Desert, desert sumac is widespread in western Texas and adjacent Chihuahua. Elsewhere in the Southwest, its distribution is interrupted. In southeastern Arizona, the plants are locally abundant on soils derived from limestone. Rivers often serve as migration corridors for plants, and, in southern New Mexico, desert sumac has made its way northward along the Rio Grande and Pecos river drainages.

Birds relish the fruits, and so do people, who sometimes make honey-sweetened tea by steeping the berries in warm water. Hot, the tea is soothing for sore throats; cold, it makes a refreshing drink for summer days.

# Desert elderberry

fruits

© Brian Wignall 93

## *Sambucus caerulea*
**Raf. var.** *mexicana* **(Presl) L. Benson**

Honeysuckle Family
Caprifoliaceae

In the desert, this big shrub or small tree generally grows with mesquites and willows in dense bosques, or floodplain woodlands. It can be found from western Texas to southern California, and far south into Mexico.

The leaves, divided into three to five saw-toothed leaflets, are distinctive, as are the broad, white-flowered inflorescences. Dozens, if not hundreds, of small flowers cluster together to make up this type of inflorescence, which is called a corymb. You might expect the pretty, delicate flowers to be sweet-scented; instead, their odor is somewhat fetid, like dirty socks. This is typical of fly-pollinated flowers. The corymb serves as a platform for flies and other insects, which, in scurrying across the cluster, pollinate the blossoms.

Desert elderberry blooms from March to June and bears its succulent blue-black berries in summer. Birds quickly denude the plants of fruits; humans who want to turn the berries into jellies, pies or wines must act quickly.

# Soapberry

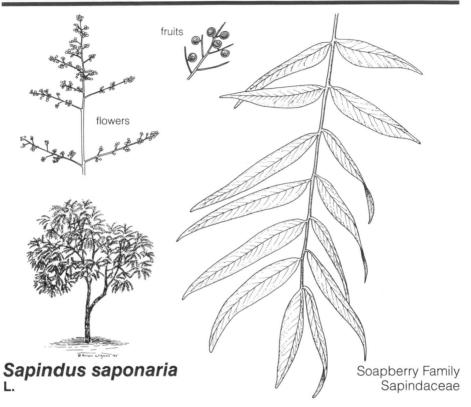

fruits

flowers

*Sapindus saponaria*
L.

Soapberry Family
Sapindaceae

The soapberry hairstreak, a chocolate-brown butterfly with delicate markings, frequents soapberry groves throughout the Southwest. During its flight period in late spring, this pretty butterfly often perches high in soapberry trees. The caterpillars eat only soapberry foliage. Adult butterflies time their emergence to coincide with the blossoming of soapberry flowers, their main source of nectar.

Soapberry can be a riparian tree forty or fifty feet tall. More often, you see it as copses of saplings along dry, sandy streambeds. The plants spread by underground rhizomes, and each copse is essentially a clone. Soapberry leaves are divided into a dozen or more lance-shaped leaflets. They look much like walnut leaves but have entire rather than toothed margins. The inconspicuous flowers produce berries about the size and color of garbanzo beans.

Ripening in summer and fall and often persisting on the trees throughout the winter, soapberries are rich in saponins, a class of compounds known for its medicinal and poisonous properties. In Mexico and the Southwest, native peoples have tossed crushed soapberries into streams to stupefy fish. They also macerated soapberries in water to make lather for washing clothes and hair.

# Banana yucca

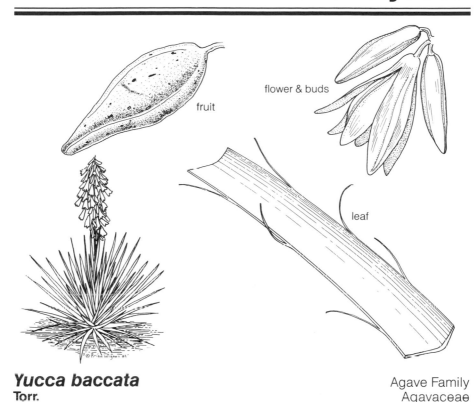

fruit

flower & buds

leaf

## *Yucca baccata*
**Torr.**

Agave Family
Agavaceae

Leaves of this yucca can be quite variable—curved or straight, bluish-green or yellowish-green, borne on a short, creeping stem or clumped on the ground. Fruits are solid, green capsules plump with succulent flesh. The capsules of most yucca species are dry. When ripe, they split open so that the seeds can fall out. Banana yucca fruits never split. The seeds are dispersed by packrats, rabbits, and other animals that eat the fruits. Several million years ago, large mammals like the giant ground sloth, now extinct, may have eaten the fruits and dispersed the seeds.

Banana yucca blooms from April to June. During its lifetime, a given plant will flower many times, unlike the agaves, which flower once, then die. Flowering and producing fruits requires a considerable expenditure of stored sugars. After a banana yucca blooms, it must recuperate for several years before it can flower again. Depending on how wet the winter has been, many plants in a population might flower in the spring, or only a few.

Banana yucca clumps may reach six feet in height, but more often they are three or four feet tall. The species grows from southern Nevada and Utah through Arizona and New Mexico into western Texas. It was once a staple food of the native peoples within its range.

# Joshua tree

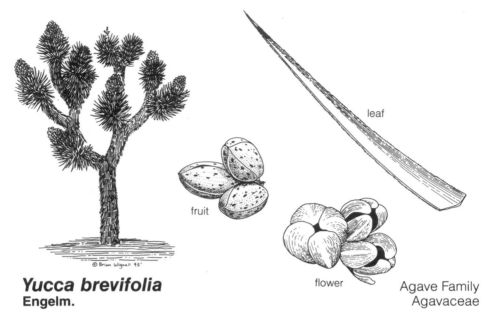

leaf

fruit

flower

## Yucca brevifolia
**Engelm.**

Agave Family
Agavaceae

Early Mormon settlers called this the Joshua tree because the plants seem to lift their arms in supplication like the Biblical Joshua. The trees are patriarchal in age as well as name. The oldest probably live for two hundred years, perhaps longer. (It is difficult to know for certain because the fibrous trunks do not form annual rings.)

Frequently the largest plants by far in their landscape, Joshua trees reach thirty to fifty feet in height and may spread to twenty feet. They branch abundantly as they age. The older the plant, the more branches it has. Young plants consist of a single stem which has one growing point. After it produces a flower stalk, the growing point dies, which means that the stem can grow no further. The plant responds by branching, that is, by sprouting a new stem near the tip of the old one. When the new stem flowers, it too will die and again a new branch will be formed. Injuries, such as insect or wind damage, also cause Joshua trees to branch. Branching enables the plants to continue their reproductive life to a very old age, unlike the agaves, which flower once, then die.

The Josuha tree is home to as many as twenty-five different species of birds. Scott's orioles hang their nests from the short, stiff leaves. Northern flickers excavate nest holes in the trunks, which other birds later occupy. Fallen branches, as they decay, are consumed by termites, which are in turn eaten by the night lizard, a shy reptile that lives under the protective cover of the Joshua tree bark.

Joshua trees are found on plains and gentle slopes from southern California to southern Nevada and western Arizona.

# Soaptree

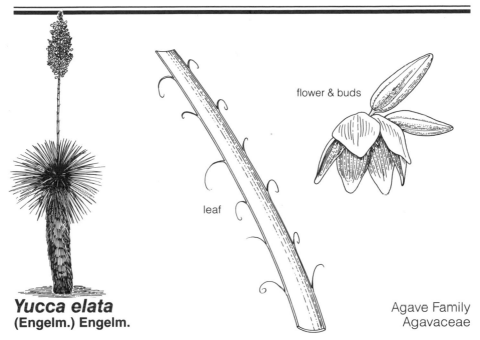

flower & buds

leaf

## *Yucca elata*
**(Engelm.) Engelm.**

Agave Family
Agavaceae

This arborescent yucca is rich in saponins, a class of chemicals that produce lather in water, thus the common name "soaptree." Native Americans have sliced the stems and roots for shampoo and soap. They have used the leaf fibers for weaving baskets, mats, sandals and nets, and they have eaten the flowers, which are rich in vitamin C. Today, cattle eat the young flower stalks. On heavily grazed rangeland, only the tallest plants are able to flower.

The rosette of narrow leaves is produced atop a trunk that may reach fifteen feet in height. Mature plants are reminiscent of miniature palm trees, thus the Spanish common name palmilla, or little palm. The long, graceful flower stalks, heavy with white, bell-shaped flowers, appear from May to July. A plant of gravelly washes and silty plains from southern Arizona to western Texas, soaptree reaches its greatest abundance in desert grassland. Here, where accumulated dead grasses provide enough fuel to carry a fire, soaptree is subject to occasional burning. The plants typically burn to the ground but then sprout from the base, producing several main trunks instead of one.

Two other species of yucca—the Great Plains yucca (*Yucca glauca* Nutt.) and narrowleaf yucca (*Yucca angustissima* Engelm.)—also have narrow, fibrous leaves and look much like soaptree except that the rosettes of leaves have no trunk. The Great Plains yucca is found from southern Wyoming to New Mexico, Texas, and the Mexican state of Chihuahua. Narrowleaf yucca is a plant of sandy soils in northern Arizona, southern Utah, and Nevada. These and related species intergrade where they grow together and can be impossible to tell apart.

# Torrey yucca

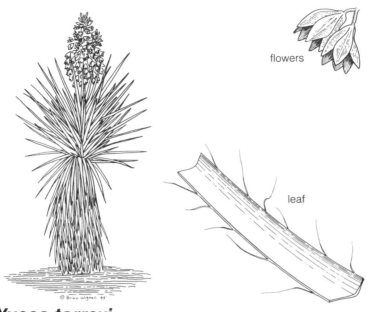

flowers

leaf

*© Brian Wignall 93*

## *Yucca torreyi*
**Schafer**

Agave Family
Agavaceae

Growing to twelve or fifteen feet tall, Torrey yucca has swordlike, yellow-green leaves. In March, April, and May, short stalks bloom with creamy, bell-shaped flowers. Each flower has three petals and three sepals, all more or less alike; botanists often call them "tepals." Sometimes the tepals are tinged with purple.

Torrey yucca, like other southwestern yuccas, is pollinated exclusively by female moths in the genus Tegeticula. After she mates, the female moth gathers a ball of pollen from the anthers of a yucca flower, then flies to a different yucca plant, where she lays her eggs on the small, green ovary inside a flower. Next she rubs the ball of pollen into the stigmas that sit atop the ovary. Later, as the seeds inside the ovary develop, the moth eggs will hatch into tiny caterpillars that eat the seeds. Although it might seem destructive, both the moth and the yucca gain by this arrangement. The flowers are ensured of pollination, and the caterpillars are guaranteed a steady food supply. Since the caterpillars eat only a fraction of the seeds inside any one capsule, there are plenty of seeds left for dispersal in late summer.

Torrey yucca, which closely resembles the Mojave yucca (*Yucca schidigera* Roezl) of southeastern California, southern Nevada and northwestern Arizona, can be found on gravelly plains and gentle slopes from central Texas into New Mexico and northern Mexico.

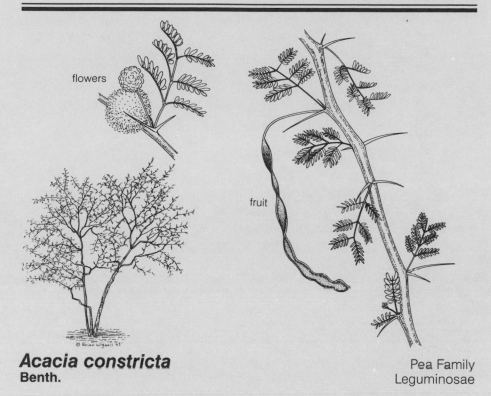

flowers

fruit

© Brian Wignall '93

## *Acacia constricta*
**Benth.**

Pea Family
Leguminosae

An individual white thorn flower is not much larger than an uppercase "A." Although insignificant as individuals, the golden yellow flowers gain importance by clustering together in tight little balls. Only a few of the flowers in each inflorescence produce fruits. The rest, which eventually fall unfertilized, are not wasted, however; they contribute to the showy display that attracts pollinators.

When white thorn flowers in spring and summer, you can smell the intensely sweet blossoms from some distance. In fact, a close relative, a subtropical species known as sweet acacia or huisache, is cultivated in France for use in perfumes. As sweet as they smell, white thorn flowers are largely neglected by insect pollinators such as butterflies and bees. Most insects quickly learn that the blossoms are attractive cheats, providing little pollen and no nectar. The shrubs often set abundant fruit anyway. Evidently they are able to lure enough naive insects to do the job.

White thorn leaves drop in response to frost or drought, and in exceptionally dry years, the plants may be leafless much of the time. Even without leaves, the five-foot-tall shrubs are readily recognized by their mahogany-colored bark and stiff, straight, white spines. White thorn thrives on rocky slopes and along washes from southern Arizona into West Texas.

# Desert agave

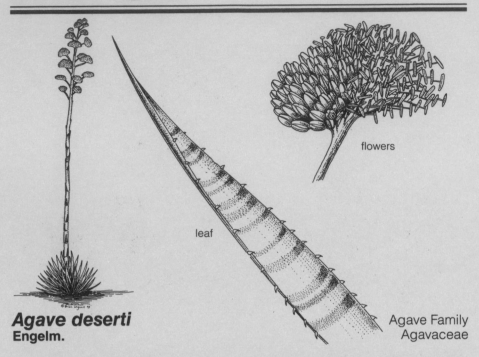

flowers

leaf

*Agave deserti*
Engelm.

Agave Family
Agavaceae

Desert agave spends most of its life as a rosette—a cluster of basal leaves. Like other agaves, it is often called century plant because its flowering is delayed. After a period of time—as long as thirty years, perhaps, but always far less than a century—an inflorescence erupts from the center of the rosette and grows at the astonishing rate of two and one-half inches a day until it reaches five to fifteen feet in height and resembles a coat-tree or hat-rack. The plant blooms for several weeks, then dies. Its death is largely a consequence of the large size of the flower stalk, which, like all plant parts, is constructed of water and carbon. In supplying water and carbon to the inflorescence, the rosette is depleted of all its resources and has no option but to die. Before this happens, however, the flowers will have been pollinated and abundant seed (up to 65,000 per stalk) produced.

Without this agave, many desert animals would be hard-pressed to survive. In the arid mountains of southwestern Arizona and southeastern California, the tough but succulent leaves are often the only water source for bighorn sheep during the driest months of the year. The yellow flowers, borne from May to July, provide nectar for hummingbirds and insects at a time of year when little else flowers. Carpenter bees tunnel into the pithy flower stalks to make their nests. The caterpillars of certain butterflies, the giant skippers, can feed on no other plant but desert agave and its montane relatives. Native peoples have also found many uses for desert agave, from baking the hearts for food to pulverizing the leaves for fiber.

# Sweetbush

## *Bebbia juncea*
### (Benth.) Greene

Sunflower Family
Compositae

Sweetbush is one of many desert shrubs that substitute green stems for green leaves. When present, the slender leaves are sparse and short-lived. Caterpillars of the Wright metalmark, a desert butterfly, specialize not on the ephemeral leaves but on the stem epidermis, the thin layer of tissue on the stem surface.

Leaflessness is a water-saving device common to a variety of desert shrubs. The advantage of stem photosynthesis is that the rate of water loss through open pores is lower. Stems have a lower surface-to-volume ratio than leaves, therefore fewer pores.

The orangish flowers of sweetbush, clustered into thimble-sized heads, appear at almost any time of year, given enough rain. They are sweetly fragrant and attract many bees and butterflies. In the absence of its distinctive flowers, sweetbush can be difficult to distinguish from other leafless shrubs. Its most notable feature is the densely packed, slender stems, which are ashy green and faintly striated. Sweetbush forms large, rounded clumps in washes, at roadsides, and on rocky slopes from southern California and Nevada into southeastern Arizona.

# Blue paloverde

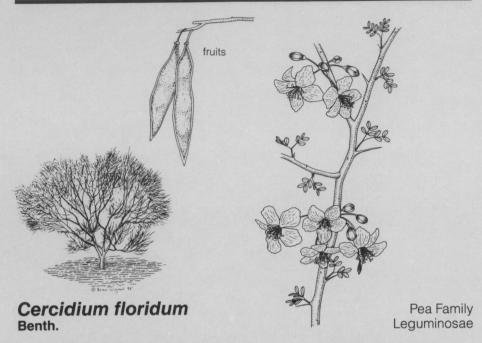

fruits

## *Cercidium floridum*
**Benth.**

Pea Family
Leguminosae

This is a graceful tree of desert washes. Only after summer rains do the small leaves appear. The rest of the year, the blue-green twigs and branches substitute for leaves in producing the sugars necessary for growth. In English, *palo verde* means "green stick."

When blue paloverde blooms in late March or April, you can hardly see the tree itself, so drenched is it in lemon yellow blossoms. Each flower comprises five yellow petals, the uppermost spotted with red. The straw-colored seed pods hang on the trees for many months after they ripen in May and June. Native Americans have ground the seeds for food. The larvae of bruchid beetles, which are dark insects not much larger than the head of a pin, also feast on the seeds. You can often see their neat little exit holes in the pods. A second species of bruchid finds these holes, enters the pods, and lays its eggs on the remaining seeds. If not for a certain tiny wasp, which parasitizes the developing beetle larvae, the annual crop of blue paloverde seeds would be severely reduced.

Blue paloverde occurs with foothill paloverde over much of southern Arizona and the Mexican state of Sonora, but the two can be easily distinguished. Foothill paloverde, as its name implies, is a plant of hills and slopes rather than washes. Its bark is yellow-green rather than blue-green; in fact, it is sometimes called yellow paloverde. The zigzag twigs of foothill paloverde are tipped with thorns; the wandlike stems of blue paloverde bear small stiff spines at the nodes.

# Foothill paloverde

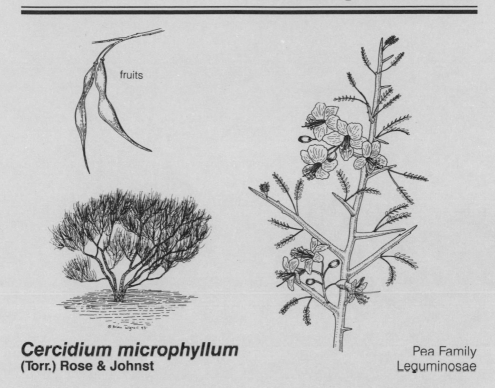

fruits

## Cercidium microphyllum
**(Torr.) Rose & Johnst**

Pea Family
Leguminosae

This small tree, one of the characteristic plants of the Sonoran Desert, dominates rocky slopes and gravelly flats from southern Arizona well into the Mexican states of Baja California and Sonora. Foothill paloverde flowers in late April or May. Each blossom has four pale yellow petals and one white one. All the trees in an area flower simultaneously, painting valleys and bajadas with yellow as far as the eye can see.

The seeds are a staple food of the many small rodents that inhabit the desert. By burying the seeds, the rodents fulfill one requirement for seed germination. The arrival of the summer rains fulfills another, and uneaten seeds germinate in surprising abundance. A large proportion of these new seedlings succumb to seasonal drought in the months of September and October. Rodents and rabbits eat many others, and most of the remainder die during the hot, dry months of May and June. The few that surive all these hazards stand a good chance of living to produce seeds of their own.

Like other green-stemmed desert plants, foothill paloverde employs its bark in photosynthesis. In fact, three-quarters of the food it manufactures is made by the bark; only one-quarter is produced by the small leaves, which appear and drop throughout the year in response to rainfall and drought. Since bark photosynthesis is inefficient, the rate of food production is low, and the trees grow slowly. A plant eighteen feet tall may be several hundred years old.

**91**

# Agritos

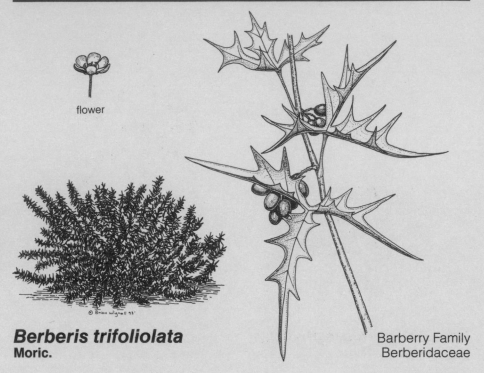

flower

### *Berberis trifoliolata*
**Moric.**

Barberry Family
Berberidaceae

Birds relish the red berries of this three- to six-foot-tall shrub. Humans might find them too sour to eat out of hand, but they do make an excellent jelly. They ripen in June and July.

If you scratch the leaf surface, you will find that its grayish color comes from a thin, waxy coat. Underneath the wax, the leaf is bright green. Waxiness serves a triple function in desert plants. By retarding water loss from the leaf surface, it enables the plants to survive periodic drought. By increasing reflectivity, it keeps leaf temperatures from rising too high. And, by creating a hard surface, it makes it difficult for rust, fungi, and other pathogens to gain a foothold.

The three-parted leaves of agritos are rigid, hard, and leathery. The botanical term for them is "sclerophyllous," which means "hard-leaved." Sclerophylly is more common among chaparral plants than desert plants. Generally, the trees and shrubs of the desert simply drop their leaves when the soil dries out or when winter temperatures plummet. Their ephemeral leaves are typically soft and pliable. In chaparral, moisture is somewhat more dependable than in desert, so shrubs can keep their leaves year-round. Still, if they are to endure cold winters and dry summers, the leaves must be tough. Agritos is widespread in central and western Texas where winters can be bitterly cold and summers uncomfortably warm.

# Rubber rabbitbrush

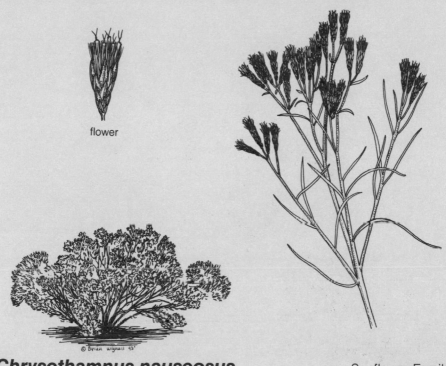

flower

## *Chrysothamnus nauseosus*
**(Pall.) Britt.**

Sunflower Family
Compositae

Rubber rabbitbrush blooms abundantly in the fall, splashing roadsides and plains with golden yellow. The wandlike, yellow-green stems are characteristic, as is their somewhat fetid odor when crushed. The Navajo have used the flowering branches to make yellow dyes. Multitudes of bees, wasps, and butterflies visit the flowers, which bloom at a time of year when few other nectar and pollen sources are available.

There are twenty-two different subspecies of rubber rabbitbrush. Some are quite distinctive in their appearance; others are hard to tell apart. Where several subspecies occur in the same general region, they tend to occupy different habitats. One might prefer mountain slopes, the other valley bottoms. One might tolerate salty soils, the other not. This kind of physical separation limits hybridization and keeps the subspecies distinct. A subspecies is an incipient species; given enough time and sufficient isolation, it may evolve into a distinct entity.

Predominantly a shrub of cold deserts and pinyon-juniper woodlands, rubber rabbitbrush is most abundant in the Great Basin. Several different subspecies occur in the greater Southwest.

# Burro fat

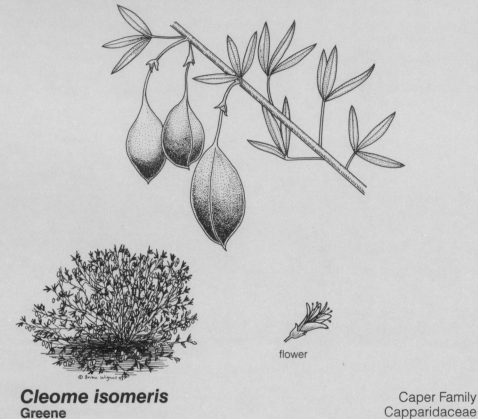

flower

© Brian Wignall 95

## *Cleome isomeris*
**Greene**

Caper Family
Capparidaceae

Burro fat, a three- to five-foot-tall shrub, is also called bladder pod after its inflated fruits, which are borne on slender stalks. Surprisingly light for their size, these papery balloons may blow readily about the landscape when ripe, thus dispersing the seeds. The spring-blooming flowers are mustard yellow, with long stamens and pistils. When rubbed or crushed, the leaves and stems smell something like dirty socks.

A small white butterfly, Becker's white (*Pieris beckerii*), lays its eggs on burro fat. You might find its green and orange larvae on the leaves in the spring. These caterpillars also eat various kinds of wild mustards (*Sisymbrium*, *Brassica*, etc.). Burro fat and wild mustard belong to different but closely related plant families, and their chemical composition is evidently similar enough that Becker's whites can thrive on both.

Burro fat has a weedy look, and indeed the plants do perform well in disturbed situations such as roadsides and sandy washes. The species is found in southern California from the coast to the desert.

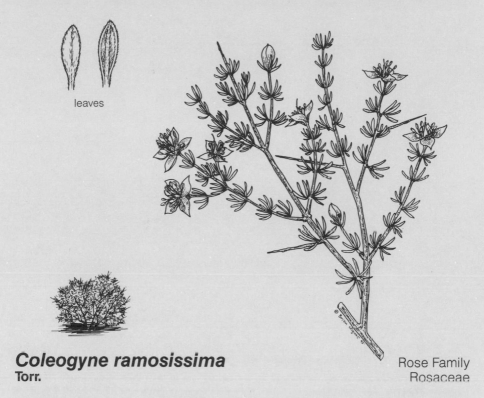

leaves

## *Coleogyne ramosissima*
**Torr.**

Rose Family
Rosaceae

Its dark gray bark makes this intricately branched shrub appear black from a distance, creating a rather somber landscape. When it blooms in April and May, however, blackbrush is quite pretty. There are no petals; the four sepals, all bright yellow on the inside, take over the function of petals, attracting pollinators to the cluster of stamens and pistil in the flower's center. The tiny leaves are gray and arise in pairs on the spine-tipped branches.

Blackbrush is not widely distributed, but where it occurs it is often dominant. It is found in a narrow band from southeastern California across southern Nevada and northern Arizona into southern Utah. The plants tend to grow where rainfall is rather high — from ten to twenty inches a year. For many desert shrubs, this is simply too much rain, but not for blackbrush, which thereby gains dominance over a large territory.

The seeds germinate only when spring rains are unusually early. Even when this uncommon event happens, most seedlings fail to survive past their first year. The result is a community in which individuals only rarely become established. But, because the shrubs grow slowly and live to a great age (well over one hundred years), the seedlings that do survive maintain their position for a long time, making it difficult for new plants to find space.

# Brittlebush

## *Encelia farinosa*
**A. Gray**

Sunflower Family
Compositae

At its best, brittlebush is a hemisphere of blue-green leaves; at its worst, it is a collection of white stems to which a few withered, gray leaves cling like bedraggled flags. The plants alternate between these two personalities on a seasonal basis. After winter rains moisten the soil, an entire canopy of new leaves replaces the old. Taking advantage of sunny days and damp soil, these leaves manufacture sugars at a rapid rate.

As the soil dries out, most leaves fall. The few that remain are small and covered with hairs pressed flat against the leaf surface. They manufacture sugars, too, but at a much lower rate, since the dense coat of hairs reflects much of the incoming sunlight. This is not a disadvantage, however; deflecting solar radiation keeps the leaves from becoming too hot and also retards water loss. These white or gray leaves cling to the stems for many months unless the soil becomes extremely dry, whereupon they also fall. Because drought induces dormancy in the stem tip, no new leaves can be produced until rains have moistened the soil once again. Then the cycle begins anew.

When brittlebush blooms in the spring, entire hillsides turn yellow. The blossoms are large for a desert plant, about the size of a half-dollar. Each contains numerous disk flowers in the central medallion and about a dozen ray flowers on the perimeter. Across most of the desert, both types of flowers are yellow, but along the lower Colorado River, the disk flowers are often dark purple. Brittlebush is found from southern California and southern Arizona into the adjacent Mexican states of Baja California and Sonora. Butterflies, moths, and small beetles pollinate the flowers.

## Encelia frutescens
(A. Gray) A. Gray

Sunflower Family
Compositae

This rounded shrub about two or three feet tall is notable for its brittle, white stems and rough, dark green leaves. Green brittlebush puts out its bright yellow, bell-shaped flower heads whenever rainfall provides the opportunity. The plants are opportunists in other ways, too. Unlike brittlebush, its grayer relative, the leaves of green brittlebush lack a dense coat of hairs. They cannot adjust their photosynthetic pace to suit the climate. When soil moisture is high, the plants produce abundant new leaves, which photosynthesize at a rapid rate, producing the sugars needed for growth. As the soil dries out, the leaves drop and the plants become dormant until the next rainfall.

Green brittlebush colonizes disturbed spots such as roadsides and washes. Although plants growing in washes are liable to be ripped out by flash floods and those at roadsides may be mowed or sprayed or trampled, green brittlebush has little choice in its habitat. Because the plants have no mechanisms to prevent excessive water loss from their leaves, they need plenty of moisture, which they get from rainfall and runoff from roadsides and washes.

The species occurs from southeastern California to eastern Arizona and north into southern Nevada and Utah.

# Cooper golden bush

© Brian Wignall 93

## *Ericameria cooperi*
**(Gray) Hall**

Sunflower Family
Compositae

Between April and June, Cooper golden bush, a low, rounded shrub to three feet tall, becomes a mass of yellow flowers. Blooming follows the winter rains, which occur more or less predictably across the range of this species. In southern Arizona, turpentine bush (*Ericameria laricifolia* [Gray] Shinners), a close relative and near-twin of Cooper golden bush, blooms in the fall. It responds to the abundant summer rains characteristic of its region.

Both species have evergreen leaves that are clustered toward the branch tips. The leaves are short, flat and narrow, a configuration that minimizes water loss. They are dotted with small resin glands, visible to the naked eye as dark pinpoints, that give off a pungent odor when crushed.

Cooper golden bush grows on rocky slopes and in crevices on bedrock outcrops from southern California into southern Nevada. Turpentine bush can be found in similar habitats from northwestern Arizona to southwestern New Mexico, and in western Texas.

# Tar bush

flower

## *Flourensia cernua*
**DC.**

Sunflower Family
Compositae

Tar bush is a four- to five-foot-tall shrub with sooty-looking bark. It some-times forms nearly pure stands on valley floors and gentle slopes. A charac-teristic species of the Chihuahuan Desert of western Texas, southern New Mexico, and northeastern Mexico, tar bush barely reaches Arizona. In the southeastern corner of that state, it grows with other Chihuahuan Desert plants like viscid acacia and desert sumac. Overgrazing by cattle may have encour-aged these desert plants, which now grow where extensive grasslands once thrived.

*Cernua* means "nodding," and refers to the yellow flower heads. If you examine them closely, you will see that there are no rays; all the flowers in the head are disk flowers. Tar bush blooms from July to October. Although the leaves turn brown when temperatures drop below freezing, they often remain on the plant throughout the winter. A new crop of leaves is produced in the spring. Resins make them somewhat shiny.

In Mexico, the leaves and flower heads are sold as a remedy for indiges-tion.

# Snakeweed

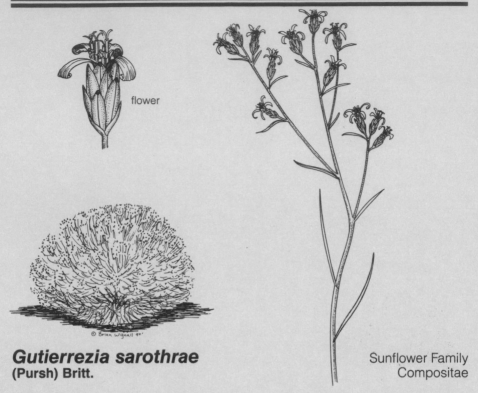

flower

## *Gutierrezia sarothrae*
**(Pursh) Britt.**

Sunflower Family
Compositae

In full flower, snakeweed is a yellow dome about two feet high. Each individual flower is miniscule, but since a dozen flowers are combined into a single head and a thousand heads may be produced by a single plant, the result is a showy display. In the autumn, entire fields and plains turn yellow as the snakeweed blooms.

Where abundant, snakeweed is one obvious sign that the land has been badly overgrazed. Since cattle eat grasses in preference to snakeweed, the latter multiply as the former decrease. Once a former grassland has been overrun by snakeweed, chances are poor that it will revert to grass. Even sheep and goats, notorious for their ability to eat just about anything, avoid snakeweed if possible.

From the point of view of a land manager or a conservationist, snakeweed is a worthless plant, not even useful in retarding soil erosion. But Hispanics and Native Americans have found several uses for snakeweed foliage, including teas for treating stomach disorders, rheumatism, and malaria; poultices for snakebite; and brooms for sweeping.

The narrow, flexible leaves have a distinctive resinous odor when crushed, and this is the source of two additional common names — resin-weed and turpentine-weed. Snakeweed occurs throughout the Southwest.

# Burro weed

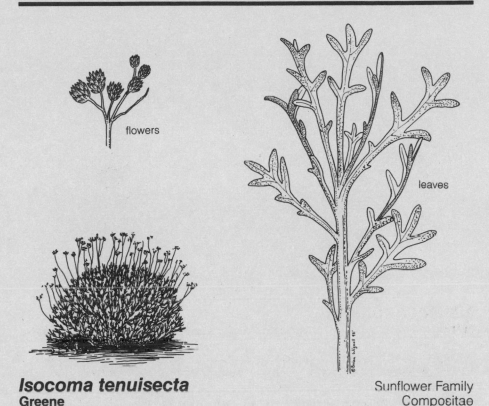

flowers

leaves

## *Isocoma tenuisecta*
**Greene**

Sunflower Family
Compositae

Burro weed foliage is poisonous, and if there is anything else for cattle to eat, they ignore it. As a result, the plants multiply on overgrazed ranges, sometimes becoming so numerous they form nearly pure stands. The same characteristics that enable burro weed to flourish on overgrazed ranges also make it a sturdy occupant of highway shoulders, parking lots, dirt roads, vacant lots, and other unpromising locales. Disturbed sites do not, in general, last long, so plants that colonize them are typically short-lived species that grow rapidly and produce abundant seed. In the case of burro weed, the seeds are small, light and wind-borne. As the original disturbance heals, at least a few seeds will find other disrupted habitats nearby.

Burro weed blooms in late summer and fall. The yellow flower heads are small but capable of a showy display when massed at the stem tips. The resinous leaves are divided into short, narrow lobes. Although this one- to three-foot-tall shrub looks like turpentine bush and acts like snakeweed, its divided leaves make it easy to recognize.

A plant of gravelly plains and gentle slopes, burro weed is found in southeastern Arizona, southern Texas, and adjacent Mexican states.

# Coulter hibiscus

flower

## *Hibiscus coulteri*
**Harv.**

Mallow Family
Malvaceae

One of the most beautiful plants of the desert, Coulter hibiscus blooms briefly at almost any time of year after rains have thoroughly moistened the soil. From a distance, the pale yellow flowers seem to float in mid-air, since the slender, straggling stems blend in with their background. Up close, you can see the red spot at the base of each petal and the brush of stamens and styles in the center.

Like many wildflowers, this one was named after its discoverer. Thomas Coulter, born in 1793, was an Irish naturalist who studied in Geneva under the great Swiss botanist August De Candolle. As much an adventurer as a scientist, Coulter accepted a position as a physician in Mexico and set sail in 1824. For the next decade, he worked and traveled in northern Mexico and southern Arizona, collecting plants wherever he went. When he finally returned to Europe, he brought along some fifty thousand specimens of pressed plants and, just as crucial, many pages of botanical manuscripts and journal notes to document his collections. Ironically, after criss-crossing the Southwest and navigating the Atlantic Ocean in perfect safety, all the papers somehow disappeared on the journey from London to Dublin. Deeply saddened by his loss and broken in health from his long travels, Coulter devoted the remaining nine years of his life to the study of his many specimens.

In southern Arizona and parts of New Mexico and western Texas, Coulter hibiscus is not uncommon on rocky slopes. The plants often seek support among the branches of foothill paloverde and other trees and shrubs.

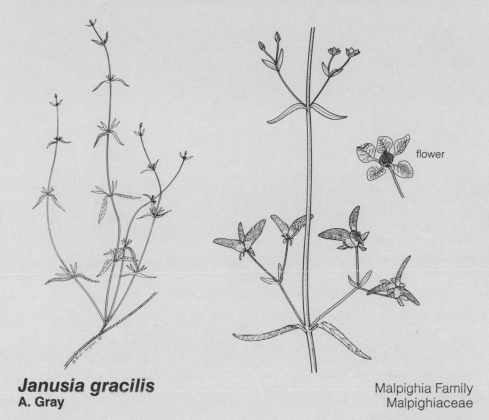

flower

## *Janusia gracilis*
**A. Gray**

Malpighia Family
Malpighiaceae

Janusia is part shrub, part vine. While the lower, woody stems are generally self-supporting, the upper, green stems twine around the stalks of nearby plants, or around one another if nothing else is available. The fruits are samaras, like maple fruits. Each seed is enclosed in a papery wing that is dispersed by wind. Janusia often clambers among the branches of paloverde and other trees and can be found on rocky slopes from southern Arizona to western Texas.

After heavy rains, small but cheerful flowers decorate the vining stems. Each flower is composed of five bright yellow petals and an equal number of inconspicuous green sepals. If you look closely at the flowers, you might be able to discern the paired glands at the base of each sepal. In almost any other flower, these would exude nectar, but in janusia they produce oil. Bees of the genus *Centris* collect oil from the glands, then combine it with pollen and use the mixture as larval food. *Centris* bees and janusia flowers demonstrate co-evolution, which means that they evolved in tandem: the bees have special scrapers on their legs for collecting the oil, and janusia, because it offers oil instead of nectar, is pollinated exclusively by *Centris* bees.

# Creosote bush

flower                        leaf     fruit

*Larrea tridentata*
**(Moc. & Sess.) Cav.**

Caltrop Family
Zygophyllaceae

The Tohono O'odham (Papago Indians) say that creosote bush is their drugstore because it provides medications for stiff limbs, sores, snake bites, menstrual cramps, and many other ills. It seems likely that the same chemicals that make creosote bush a veritable drugstore also render it unpalatable to insects and mammals, for very few animals can consume the resinous foliage without ill effect. Exceptions include a small desert grasshopper and a walking stick that have have adapted so thoroughly to creosote bush foliage that they eat nothing else.

Although the foliage is meant to repel, the yellow flowers are not, and when creosote bush blooms in the spring, a multitude of insects, including one hundred different species of bees, visit the blossoms. Twenty-two of these are totally dependent upon creosote bush for pollen and nectar, and their springtime emergence from underground burrows and nests is timed to coincide with the creosote bush bloom. Given sufficient rainfall, the flowers can appear at other seasons, too.

An abundant shrub of gravelly plains, sandy flats, and rocky slopes from southern California to western Texas, creosote bush is the quintessential desert plant. The resins on the leaves help prevent water loss, as does the plant's habit of dropping some leaves during dry periods. Creosote bush can continue to manufacture the sugars needed for growth long after the dryness of the soil has forced other plants into dormancy. When rainfall renews soil moisture, creosote bush responds rapidly with new stems and leaves.

Creosote bush lives to a great age. As the older stems in the center of the plant die, new stems arise on the perimeter. The resulting ring of stems, essentially a clone of the original plant, can easily survive for a hundred years or more.

# Engelmann prickly pear

fruits

flower

## *Opuntia engelmannii*
**Salm-Dyck**

Cactus Family
Cactaceae

Engelmann prickly pear, an abundant cactus of flats and slopes through-out the Southwest and northern Mexico, blooms in April and May. Its many-petaled, teacup-shaped flowers are brilliant yellow when they open about eight o'clock in the morning; by the time they close in the late afternoon, they have faded to a soft apricot color. Each flower lasts only one day. The abundant pollen is avidly collected by many different kinds of insects, but only a few of them are large enough to be effective pollinators. As a bee wriggles through the mass of stamens to the nectar deep inside the flower, she becomes thoroughly dusted with pollen. The stamens themselves assist this process by twisting and curling inward over the bee. When she visits the next prickly pear flower, she brushes against the green stigmas, depositing some of the pollen she has collected.

The pads of prickly pears, actually highly modified stems, serve as water storage organs. They also substitute for leaves in the food-producing process called photosynthesis. In cacti, this involves taking up carbon dioxide by night, storing it in the form of plant acids, then turning the acids into sugars the following day. Cacti need to absorb as much sunlight as possible if they are to be efficient food-producers. Engelmann prickly pear enhances its efficiency by orienting its pads to face the sun during the time of most active growth, the summer rainy season.

Javelina, coyote, desert tortoise, and other animals feast on the sweet fruits. The cactus candy sold in souvenir shops is often made from prickly pears.

# Pygmy cedar

flower

*Peucephyllum schottii*
A. Gray

Sunflower Family
Compositae

Although it is evergreen and has needlelike leaves, this three- to four-foot-tall shrub isn't a conifer. The bell-shaped heads of yellow flowers, which appear from March to June, betray its membership in the sunflower family.

Pygmy cedar seems only marginally suited to the harsh environment of the desert. It isn't nearly as drought-tolerant as creosote bush, for example, which is why it tends to grow in washes and in cracks on cliffs. And, because the foliage suffers frost damage quite readily, the plants are restricted to the warmest parts of the southwestern desert, from southeastern California and southern Nevada into western Arizona. Pygmy cedar does show some adaptation to an arid environment, however; the needlelike shape of the leaves reduces leaf surface area to a minimum, thus retarding water loss.

# Paperdaisy

*Psilostrophe cooperi*
(A. Gray) Greene

Sunflower Family
Compositae

Paperdaisy blooms in response to good winter or summer rains. The one-foot-tall plants form hemispheres of yellow on dirt roads, highway shoulders, and other disturbed places from southeastern California and southern Nevada to Arizona and westernmost New Mexico. Measuring an inch or two in length, the narrow leaves are woolly with felt-like hairs. The name "paperdaisy" comes from the ray flowers, which turn papery and persist even after they have been bleached by the sun.

# Yellow trumpet flower

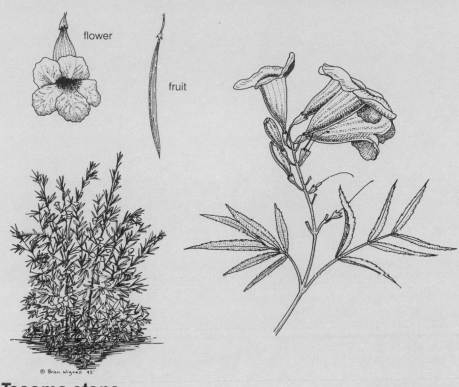

flower

fruit

© Brian Wignall 93'

## Tecoma stans
**(L.) Juss.**

Bignonia Family
Bignoniaceae

Widespread plants used in folk medicine tend to have many common names, and yellow trumpet flower is no exception. Long employed by *curanderas* to treat syphilis and diabetes, yellow trumpet flower is known in different parts of Mexico as trompetilla, tronadora, gloria, esperanza, flor de San Pedro and palo de arco. In the Southwest, it is sometimes called yellow elder because the foliage resembles elderberry leaves. The big, trumpet-shaped, yellow flowers and long, narrow seed capsules are quite distinctive, however.

This is basically a tropical species that stretches from South America, where it is a small tree up to twenty-five feet tall, to the southwestern United States, where it is a many-stemmed shrub not much more than five feet in height. The plants are killed to the ground when temperatures drop more than a few degrees below freezing, yet they also require ample moisture during the warm months. In southern Arizona and southwestern Texas, where yellow trumpet flower reaches its northern limits, the shrubs can be found in rocky canyons, where they find sufficient moisture to support luxuriant summer growth and enough protection from frost to stay alive during the winter.

# Spiny senna

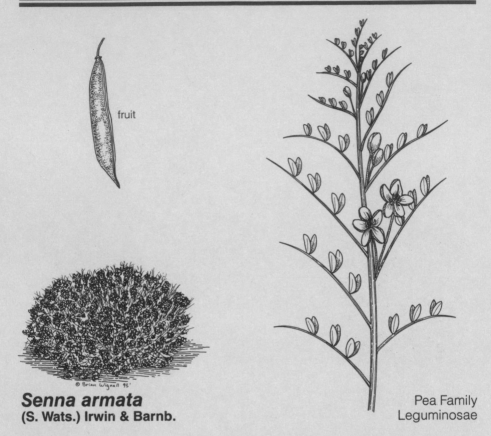

fruit

*Senna armata*
(S. Wats.) Irwin & Barnb.

Pea Family
Leguminosae

In the tropical parts of Mexico and Central America, sennas are graceful trees with luxuriantly leafy canopies and brilliant yellow flower clusters. In adapting to the arid deserts of southeastern California, spiny senna, a two-foot-tall shrub, has kept the yellow flowers and discarded the rest. Since water is a scarce commodity in deserts, many desert plants, spiny senna among them, produce only ephemeral leaves. They rely on their green stems to do the work of photosynthesis, producing the sugars necessary for growth.

In the spring, the bare stems put out flowering shoots adorned with pretty yellow flowers and sparse leaves. Each leaf is composed of four to six paired leaflets that drop within a month or two. Afterwards, the leaf axis remains as a feeble spine. Spininess is common among desert plants; no one is quite sure why. Defense against herbivores is one suggestion. Another is that spininess is a consequence of the arid environment. What is certain is that desert plants arrive at spininess by several different routes. Some, like catclaw and white thorn, develop spines by modification of tiny leaf bracts called stipules. Others, like spiny senna, press the leaf stalk or the leaf axis into service.

fruit

## Senna wislizenii
**(A. Gray) Irwin & Barnb.**

Pea Family
Leguminosae

A beautiful plant in flower, shrubby senna blooms during the summer rainy season. Each yellow blossom consists of five cupped petals surrounding a cluster of ten stamens and a single pistil. If you look at the stamens through a magnifying glass, you can see a hole in the tip of each anther. This is where the pollen comes out. To release their pollen, senna flowers must be laboriously "milked." When bees land on the blossoms, they clasp the stamens and vibrate their flight muscles until the pollen sifts out of the little holes. Often you can hear bees buzzing while they work senna flowers.

Shrubby senna often occurs on limestone and is scattered from western Texas to southeastern Arizona. The plants grow to nine feet tall and lose their leaves during periods of drought and cold.

# Trixis

flowers

### *Trixis californica*
Kellogg

Sunflower Family
Compositae

With its numerous yellow flowers and bright green foliage, trixis is a striking plant when it blooms after winter or summer rains. The plants are generally low—little more than twelve or eighteen inches tall—but they sometimes spread to twice that in width. The leaves fall in response to cold or drought, revealing the brittle, white stems.

Trixis often grows tucked at the bases of trees or among large boulders. In sheltered habitats like these, it gains some protection from frost. Even so, the plants may freeze to the ground in the coldest winters.

Trixis extends from southern California to western Texas and well south into Mexico.

# Golden-eye

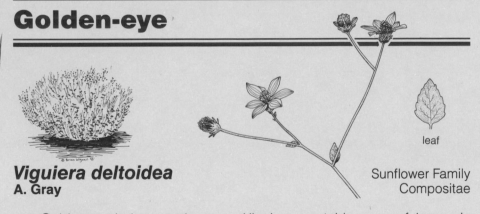

leaf

### *Viguiera deltoidea*
A. Gray

Sunflower Family
Compositae

Golden-eye belongs to the genus *Viguiera*, a notably successful group in the Southwest. There are *Viguiera* species for every altitude, from low deserts to high mountains, and for many different habitats, from rich soil in pine forests to slender cracks in boulder outcrops. Desert species include *Viguiera reticulata* S. Wats., which closely resembles brittlebush and grows in Death Valley and vicinity; *Viguiera stenoloba* Blake, a Chihuahuan Desert shrub with divided leaves; *Viguiera microphylla* Vasey & Rose, which has tiny leaves and is common in parts of Baja California; and several others.

# Desert honeysuckle

fruit

## Anisacanthus thurberi
(Torr.) A. Gray

Acanthus Family
Acanthaceae

As a hummingbird probes the brick-red flowers of desert honeysuckle, its throat picks up yellow pollen from the protruding anthers. Then, when the bird visits the next blossom, its throat brushes against the stigma, dusting it with pollen. Flowers pollinated by hummingbirds typically share certain characteristics, including red color, long floral tubes, abundant nectar and turned-back petals. This ornithophilous syndrome, as it is called, deters bees and butterflies, many of whom cannot see red and do not have tongues long enough to reach the nectar at the bottom of the floral tube. Desert honeysuckle does not quite fit the mold: the markedly short flower tube permits visits by solitary bees and other insects, and the flowers, being more orange than red, are visible to a variety of insects. Evidently desert honeysuckle straddles the fence between insect pollination and bird pollination.

Desert honeysuckle flowers appear in the spring about the same time as new leaves. Unlike many desert shrubs, desert honeysuckle is cold-deciduous rather than drought-deciduous and retains its leaves until the first hard frost. Even when the plants are not in flower, the shreddy bark and opposite leaves make the plants easy to recognize in their streambed habitat.

# Indian mallow

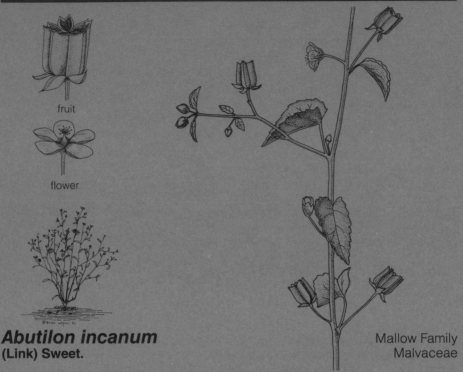

fruit

flower

## *Abutilon incanum*
**(Link) Sweet.**

Mallow Family
Malvaceae

This sparsely branched shrub is well-prepared for life in the desert. The small size of the leaves makes them resistant to water loss, as does their velvety coat of hairs. Under magnification, the interlocking hairs are shaped like asterisks. The species name *incanum*, which means hoary, comes from these velvety hairs. As in many desert shrubs, the dense hairs deflect a certain proportion of the incoming sunlight, which keeps leaf temperatures from mounting on the hottest days.

Indian mallow flowers appear after spring or summer rains and vary from pink to lavender to orange. Sometimes there is a bright maroon dot at the base of each petal. These dots show flower visitors—most often small solitary bees—where to find nectar. The bottlebrush in the center of the flower is a mass of anthers clustered around the styles. Bees collect pollen as they circle the anther column or hunch over it. In the process, they dust the stigmas with pollen, thus fertilizing the ovary.

The pale gray, woody stems of Indian mallow are usually not much thicker than a pencil. In Arizona, New Mexico and Texas, the plants are typically a foot or two tall, but in coastal Sonora, where winters are milder and summers are wetter, they may reach three or four feet in height. While never a conspicuous element of desert vegetation, Indian mallow is not uncommon on rocky slopes. It blooms in response to winter and summer rains.

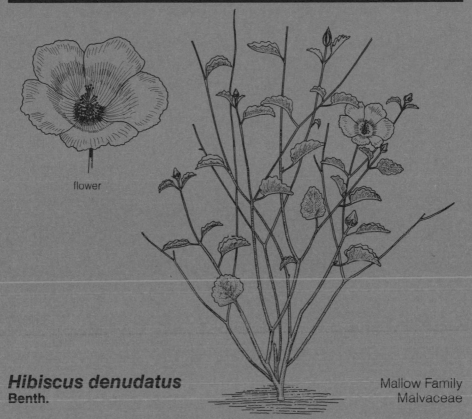

flower

## *Hibiscus denudatus*
**Benth.**

Mallow Family
Malvaceae

Of the three hundred species of hibiscus, most are tropical plants with lush foliage and generous flowers. A few species, desert hibiscus among them, have adapted to more arid environments. Reduction in leaf size is one way that desert hibiscus has accommodated itself to a dry climate, since small leaves lose less water than big ones. Another adaptation is the dense coat of hairs on the leaves and stems. By keeping air currents away from the leaf surface, the hairs slow the rate of water loss. By reflecting incoming sunlight, they lower the temperature of the leaves. During the driest, hottest months, desert hibiscus sheds its leaves entirely. This habit is the source of its Latin name, denudatus, which means denuded or naked.

Desert hibiscus is a small shrub not much more than a foot tall. The lavender flowers, shaped like teacups, are tinged with red at the center. The foliage is grayish from the hairs; if you look at them under magnification, you can see that each one is tufted like a spiny sea urchin. Desert hibiscus thrives on rocky slopes and gravelly plains from southeastern California to southeastern Arizona, and in the adjacent Mexican states of Baja California and Sonora. There are scattered populations in New Mexico and southern Texas as well.

# Fairy duster

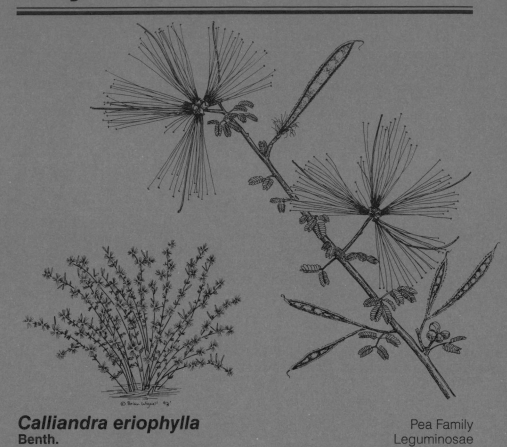

## *Calliandra eriophylla*
**Benth.**

Pea Family
Leguminosae

This lovely, pink-flowered shrub seems to bring out the romantic in its namers. In Arizona and California it is called "fairy duster," and in parts of Mexico, it is known as *cabeza angel*, which means "angel head." Even the scientific name evinces a touch of poetry: *Calliandra* means "beautiful stamen." The scientific name is accurate as well as romantic, since it is the hundreds of pink stamens in every flower head that attract our attention.

They attract the attention of insect pollinators, too, including springtime butterflies, which flutter against the stamens and carry away pollen packets on their wings. An individual fairy duster flower is a small and inconspicuous object unlikely to tempt a bee or butterfly. Its strategy is to unite with others to make a showy display. In this way, the whole is greater than the sum of its parts. Only a few of the many flowers in a head eventually produce fruits.

Fairy duster blooms in the spring, starting in February in the low desert near the Colorado River and finishing in April in the desert grasslands of southeastern Arizona.

# Feather plume

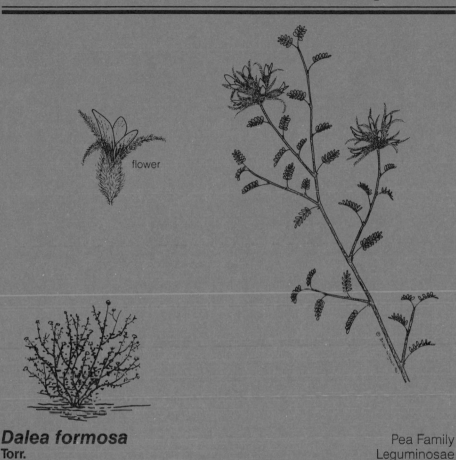

flower

## *Dalea formosa*
**Torr.**

Pea Family
Leguminosae

The diminutive size of this intricately branched shrub makes the magenta flower clusters seem outsized, like blossoms on a bonsai plant. Four to six of the narrow flowers make a cluster. The calyx, the tubular cup that contains the petals, is adorned with five feathery plumes, which give the plant its common name. The scientific name, *formosa*, is equally appropriate, for it means beautiful.

Feather plume occupies a variety of climatic zones. In southeastern Arizona, where it often grows on limestone in desert grassland and oak woodland, it is a plant of semi-arid climates. In western Texas and adjacent Mexican states, it drops down into the desert zone. In the mountains of New Mexico and Colorado, feather plume grows where the ground freezes during the winter. This adaptability comes about through ecotypic differentiation, the evolution of particular forms to suit different circumstances. The various forms look more or less alike, but their genetic make-up is quite distinct.

# Coral bean

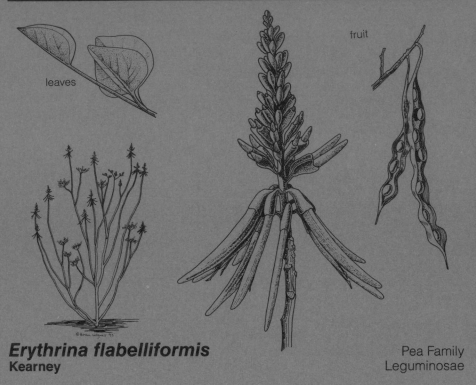

leaves

fruit

*Erythrina flabelliformis*
**Kearney**

Pea Family
Leguminosae

Everything about coral bean is distinctive and somewhat surprising. The lumpy, brown pods split to reveal a row of highly poisonous vermilion seeds. The tan, spiny stems, apparently lifeless for six months of the year, burst into bloom at the hottest, driest time of year. The three-parted leaves, which seem far too large for a desert plant, burgeon with the summer rains and last until autumn, when they blaze yellow and gold on hillsides and canyon slopes.

Coral bean flowers are well adapted for hummingbird pollination. Their red color, one that hummingbirds have learned to associate with nectar, is invisible to bees and many butterflies. Hummingbirds can easily reach the nectar, which accumulates at the base of the long floral tubes, whereas shorter tongued insects cannot. Moreover, the blossoms present no obvious foothold, a disadvantage for insects, but no problem for hummingbirds, which, of course, can hover as they feed.

The stems and leaves are frost-tender, so the plants typically grow among rocks and boulders, which absorb heat during sunny winter days and reradiate it during chilly winter nights. In this way, coral bean obtains a measure of protection from frost. Even so, the stems may freeze to the ground in the coldest winters. In southern Arizona, coral bean is a shrub up to four or five feet tall. In the Mexican state of Sonora, where winters are milder, it is a slender tree.

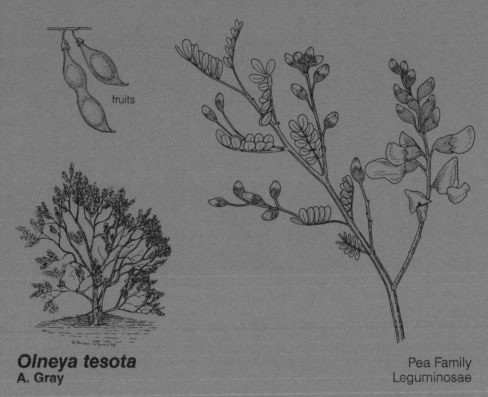

fruits

## Olneya tesota
A. Gray

Pea Family
Leguminosae

When ironwood blooms in May or June, pink to lavender blossoms cover the trees for a week or two. A variety of bees and hummingbirds devote themselves to the flowers, resulting in an abundant crop of bumpy pods containing a few purplish-brown seeds. Because ironwood seeds, unlike those of many desert legumes, lack a hard and durable seed coat, they need not wait a year or two before germinating. As soon as summer rains come, seedlings pop out of the ground, making a green shadow under every ironwood tree.

Though their flowers are short-lived, the trees themselves reach a great age. Even dead, they last a long while due to the durability and hardness of the wood. Because it is so hard, ironwood burns slowly and makes excellent coals. Scri Indians of coastal Sonora use saws, files, hatchets, and sandpaper to shape ironwood into wonderfully stylized figurines of turtles, whales, pelicans, sea lions, and other animals. Once a common and characteristic feature of the Sonoran Desert, dead ironwood snags are becoming ever rarer as the wood is harvested for fuel and art.

Ironwood is sensitive to frost, and citrus growers have long used the trees as indicators of frost-free locations for orange, lemon and grapefruit orchards. It grows in washes in Arizona, southeastern California and adjacent Mexico.

# Ocotillo

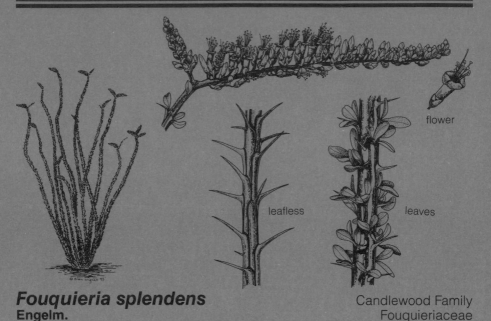

flower

leafless

leaves

*Fouquieria splendens*
**Engelm.**

Candlewood Family
Fouquieriaceae

Most of the year, the long, graceful stems of ocotillo are quite bare except for the rigid gray spines. Given a good rainstorm, this changes literally over-night as tiny new leaf buds burst all along the stem. Within five days, the leaves expand to their full size; within five weeks, they turn yellow and drop. In the meantime, they take advantage of the newly wet soil to produce the sugars necessary for growth. Depending on the rains, a plant may gain and lose its leaves six or more times a year, although three or four are more usual.

Under their waxy gray surface, ocotillo stems are chlorophyllous — pos-sessing the plant pigment chlorophyll — so they are capable of photosynthesis themselves. Stem photosynthesis produces only a small volume of sugars, but it is enough to enable the plants to leaf out quickly after rains.

Ocotillo flowers — blood-red and densely clustered at the stem tips — are gorgeous. Appearing in March and April, they are an important food source for hummingbirds during their northward migration from Mexico into the moun-tains of the West. Big, black carpenter bees also visit the flowers, as do many smaller bees, hoverflies, orioles, finches, verdins, and warblers.

The flat, featherlight seeds are produced in abundance in May and June. Although many may germinate during the summer rainy season, few if any survive until the following summer. Those that make it to their second year stand a good chance of living up to two centuries.

Ocotillo grows to a height of twenty or thirty feet and occurs abundantly from southeastern California into western Texas, and south into northern Mexico.

# Desert willow

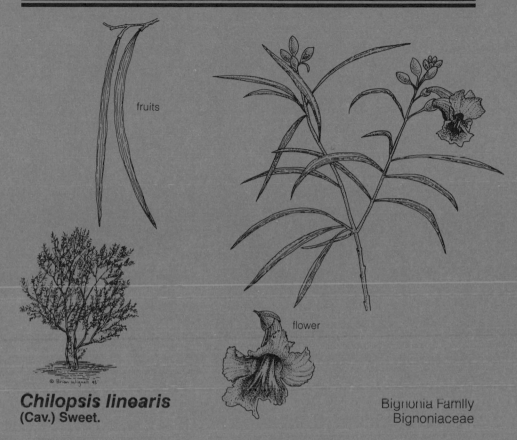

fruits

flower

## Chilopsis linearis
**(Cav.) Sweet.**

Bignonia Family
Bignoniaceae

Although this twenty-foot-tall tree is called "desert willow," no true willow ever had such big pink and lavender flowers nor such elongated seed pods dangling like brown ribbons from the gray twigs. Desert willow is, rather, a member of a large tropical family represented in the United States by only a few species. In its habit and its habitat, though, desert willow could be regarded as the dryland equivalent of true willows: it, too, grows in floodplains and washes and drops its leaves in the autumn.

Desert willow survives where true willows cannot by a complement of arid-adapted characteristics. The roots extend fifty feet or more into the ground in search of water. A waxy coating on the leaves prevents loss of moisture through the leaf surface. When summer temperatures rise too high and summer drought extends too long, desert willow drops its leaves and becomes dormant. Then, once the summer rains begin, the tree sprouts new leaves and resumes photosynthesis.

Desert willow blooms late in the spring and sometimes again in summer. Large, black carpenter bees are the main pollinators.

# Beavertail

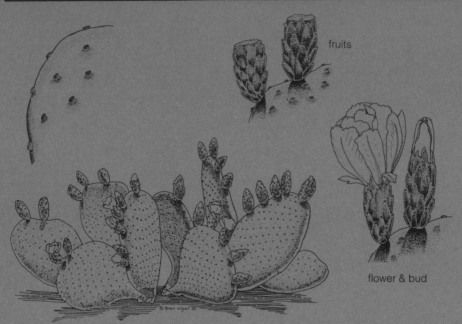

fruits

flower & bud

## *Opuntia basilaris*
**Engelm. & Bigel.**

Cactus Family
Cactaceae

Brilliant magenta flowers and blue-gray pads are the signal characteristics of the beavertail, a prickly pear found on stony flats and rocky slopes from southern Utah and western Arizona to southeastern California and northwestern Mexico. Although the pads lack the typical cactus spines, they are abundantly furnished with tiny barbs called glochids. Newly formed pads and flower buds exude dots of nectar, attracting swarms of ants. The ants collect the nectar and prey upon insects that might otherwise suck or chew the succulent cactus pads.

Only a few species of cacti are found in the most arid portions of the North American desert. Since most cacti cannot remove water from cold soils, winter is the dormant season and summer is the time of active growth. In the low-lying desert near the head of the Gulf of California, summers are too dry for most cacti, and the sparse winter rains do them little good. Moreover, severe droughts periodically threaten the existence of every plant and animal in the region. Beavertail is one of the few cactus species that thrives under these formidable conditions. During dry months, the plants lose water from their water-storage tissues before they surrender it from their photosynthetic tissues. This lets them produce sugars even when the soil is dry. It also helps keep photosynthetic tissue alive and ready to function as soon as rain moistens the soil.

# Jumping cholla

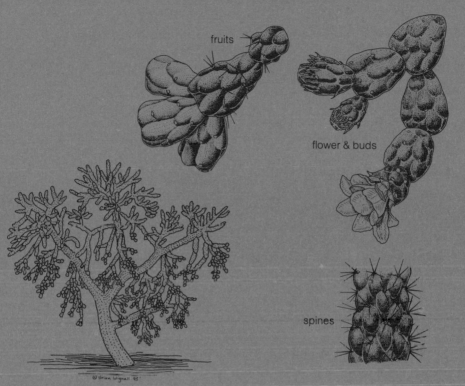

fruits

flower & buds

spines

© Brian Wignall 95

## *Opuntia fulgida*
**Engelm.**

Cactus Family
Cactaceae

Jumping cholla does not really jump, of course, despite its threatening name. The spiny joints are only loosely attached to the parent plant, and when a person or animal brushes against them, the joints readily catch in skin, fur, clothing, or boots. This is, in fact, the main way that jumping cholla disperses itself from place to place. When detached from its parent plant, a jumping cholla joint anchors itself to the soil with adventitious roots. With the arrival of summer or winter rains, it produces new joints and becomes a self-sufficient plant. Proliferating by means of fallen joints, jumping chollas can form vast, formidable thickets on plains and gentle slopes in southern Arizona and in the Mexican states of Sonoran and Sinaloa.

Jumping cholla is also called chainfruit cholla after its long chains of fruits, sometimes twenty or more growing one out of another. Since the fruits are generally sterile, it is much more common for a fallen fruit to take root and produce a new plant vegetatively than it is for seeds inside the fruit to germinate and grow.

# Staghorn cholla

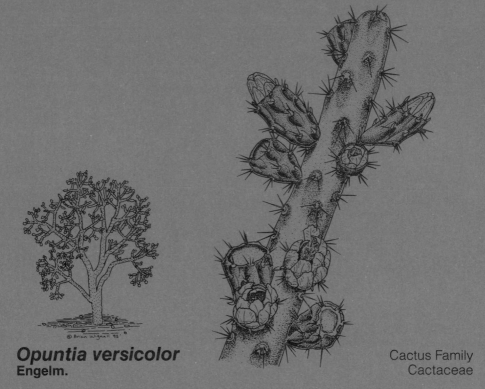

© Brian Wignall '93

## *Opuntia versicolor*
**Engelm.**

Cactus Family
Cactaceae

Sometimes reaching eight or ten feet in height, this cactus has a single trunk and a highly branched crown of cylindrical joints. Normally dull green in color, these turn reddish when exposed to cold or other environmental stresses. Flower color is also variable: some plants have rusty-red flowers, others yellow or bronze. The species name *versicolor*, which means "changing color," might refer to the joints, the flowers or both. The fruits are fleshy and remain on the branches for at least a year.

Over the course of a night and a day, staghorn cholla joints droop just a bit, then become erect again. These movements, which are too gradual to be noticeable, occur as the stems lose moisture at night and gain it back during the day. Most leafy plants do the reverse. During the day, when the sun is shining, they manufacture the sugars needed for growth and, at the same time, lose water to the atmosphere through pores in their leaves. Staghorn chollas (and other cacti), by opening their pores at night, manage to conserve precious moisture.

Staghorn cholla is found in southern Arizona. Similar, more widely distributed, species include tree cholla (*Opuntia imbricata* [Haw.] DC.) and cane cholla (*Opuntia spinosior* [Engelm.] Toumey).

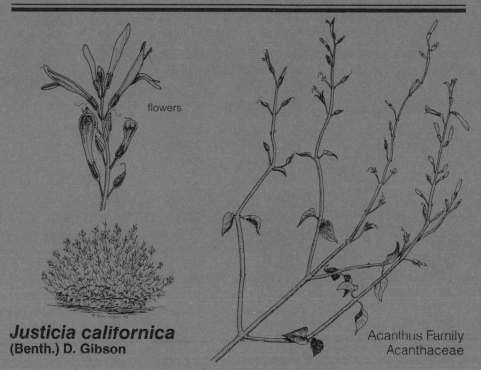

flowers

## Justicia californica
(Benth.) D. Gibson

Acanthus Family
Acanthaceae

The blooming period of chuparosa is brief but spectacular. In late February and early March, the shrubs become five-foot mounds of red, a trumpet blast of color in sandy washes from southeastern California to southwestern Arizona. The slender leaves, which appear about the same time as the flowers, are discarded when the soil dries out. Much of the year, the plants are leafless. Along with ocotillo, chuparosa is a major food source for hummingbirds during their spring migration from Mexico to the mountains of the western United States.

Chuparosa flowers are ornithophilous, which, taken literally, means "bird-loving." Taken figuratively, ornithophily refers to a complement of characteristics that attract birds, in this case hummingbirds. These include red color (which hummingbirds associate with food) and a long, slender floral tube containing abundant nectar. The ornithophilous system is designed both to attract hummingbirds, which pollinate the blossoms as they move from plant to plant, and to deter small bees and wasps, whose tongues are too short to reach the nectar.

Certain intelligent insects, like the bulbous, black carpenter bee, have learned to short-circuit this system despite its built-in precautions. Carpenter bees land on top of the floral tube, then use their sharp mouth-parts to slit the flower just above the base. This gives them access to the nectar inside, but, since they do not pollinate the flowers in return, they are nectar thieves.

# White ratany

flower

**_Krameria grayi_**
**Rose & Painter**

Ratany Family
Krameriaceae

White ratany, a spreading shrub about two feet tall, looks like many desert shrubs in its thorn-tipped stems and gray foliage. Unlike most desert plants, though, white ratany is parasitic. It attaches itself to the roots of common shrubs like creosote bush and triangle-leaf bursage and siphons off a portion of the food they manufacture for themselves. It also takes water and perhaps other nutrients from its hosts.

White ratany flowers are beautiful in their own way. Instead of being green and inconspicuous as in most flowers, the sepals are red-violet and showy. The actual petals are scarcely noticeable, and two have been so highly modified they do not resemble petals at all. They look more like glands, which is exactly what they are. Where most flowers offer nectar as a reward for pollinators, white ratany offers oil, and bees in the genus _Centris_ collect oil from the glands. The bees combine the oil with pollen from other plants, then use the mixture as larval food.

Locally common on gravelly plains and rocky slopes, white ratany occurs from southern California to western Texas. A related shrub, range ratany (_Krameria parvifolia_ Benth.), covers much the same territory. They differ mainly in characters of the plump, prickly fruits.

# Tamarisk

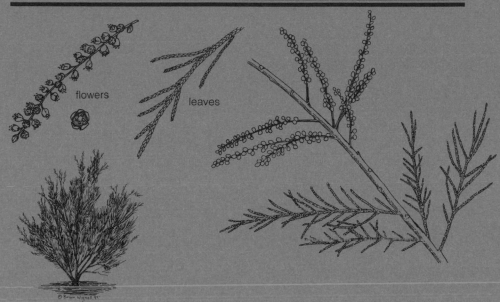

flowers

leaves

## *Tamarix ramosissima*
**Ledeb.**

Tamarisk Family
Tamaricaceae

.Thickly planted tamarisk trees make windbreaks along fields and high-ways, honeybees love the pink or white flowers, and mourning doves and other birds shelter in the foliage. Otherwise, tamarisk has probably done more harm than good since it was introduced into the United States from Eurasia.

In the Southwest, tamarisk is a riparian tree that thrives in the artificial flow regimes created by hydroelectric dams. As dams proliferated throughout the western United States, so did tamarisk. Now it is nearly impossible to find a major river in the Southwest that is not thickly lined with this fast-growing plant, which has multiplied at the expense of native riparian trees like mesquite, willow, ash, and cottonwood.

One secret of its success is prolific seed production, literally tens of thousands of seeds per tree each year. Another is timing. Dispersed in May and June, the seeds germinate on wet soil along rivers and lakes. By the time summer rains arrive, bringing higher flows, the seedlings are well-enough es-tablished to resist uprooting. Mature trees also resist flooding; their roots can survive up to three months of immersion. Moreover, by excreting excess salt from glands on the leaves and young twigs, tamarisk can survive on soils that are too salty for most native trees. (The salt crystals make whiskers on the foliage, giving rise to the common name of saltcedar.)

Several different species of tamarisk occur along southwestern rivers and lakes. They are difficult to tell apart. Many people are severely allergic to tama-risk pollen, which is produced in March and April when the flowers bloom.

# Arrow weed

fruit    flower

## *Tessaria sericea*
### (Nutt.) Shinners

Sunflower Family
Compositae

Arrow weed's narrow, lance-shaped leaves and slender, flexible stems are reminiscent of some silvery-leaved willow, but it is a member of the Sunflower Family. Like the true willows, arrow weed is a riparian plant. It is most common along the major rivers of the Southwest such as the Colorado, the Gila and the Rio Grande, where it forms thickets on sand bars, beaches and dunes.

Dense colonies are created as the underground, horizontal stems send up leafy shoots. Each colony is a clone — a single genetic individual. Clonal growth enables a species to aggressively invade and occupy suitable habitat as it opens up. Although these shallowly rooted colonies are easily ripped out by floods, the species as a whole profits from occasional periods of high water. Floods deposit fresh sand, and arrow weed is among the first colonizers of barren sand bars and beaches.

As the common name suggests, native peoples have used arrow weed in making weaponry. The straightness of the stems also has made them useful in building houses and ramadas, and their flexibility has made them invaluable for basketry.

The pale, pinkish flowers, clustered in thimble-shaped heads, appear mostly in the spring.

# Dune peabush

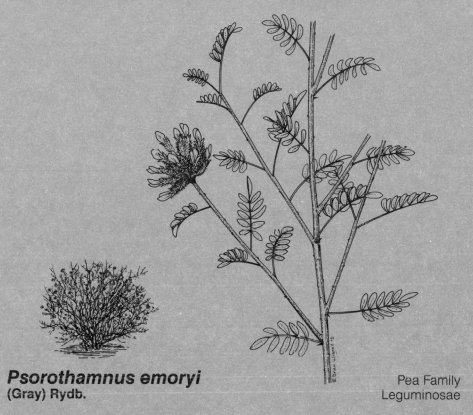

## *Psorothamnus emoryi*
**(Gray) Rydb.**

Pea Family
Leguminosae

The many species of peabush in the Southwest have diversified to occupy every possible habitat except open water. This particular peabush, a sprawling shrub to three feet high, loves sand and can be found on dunes and sandy flats in southeastern California and along the lower Colorado and Gila rivers in western Arizona.

Wind and sand movement make dunes a difficult environment for plants and animals, especially plants, which are always being overwhelmed or undermined. Some, like dune peabush, restrict themselves to areas where the sand is less active, such as stable dunes at the edges of large, active dune fields. The white, felty hairs of the leaves and stems are characteristic of dune plants: thick pubescence lowers leaf temperatures by deflecting much of the abundant sunlight.

Dune peabush is one of several hosts to sand food, a curious parasitic plant that pokes above the sand in the spring. Its mushroomlike heads lay flat on the sand and bear numerous tiny lavender flowers. The heads connect to the host plant via long rhizomes that reach down into the sand for many feet. Sand food is a rare plant and should not be collected or disturbed.

# Indigo bush

fruit

## *Psorothamnus fremontii*
**(Torr.) Barnb.**

Pea Family
Leguminosae

A straggling shrub to four feet tall, indigo bush is stiffly branched but not especially thorny. The stems of older plants are often picturesquely gnarled or twisted. When in flower, this is one of the most beautiful shrubs of the desert. Ranging in color from dark blue to deep purple, the silky blossoms contrast vividly with the whitish, zigzag stems. Often the spring-blooming flowers appear while the stems are leafless. The small leaves, divided into several pairs of leaflets, drop during periods of drought and cold.

This species was named after John C. Frémont, explorer, presidential candidate, territorial governor of Arizona, and self-taught collector of plants. He discovered indigo bush in what he called "Piute Country, California," in 1855; doubtless he was somewhere in the Mojave Desert. A shameless self-promoter, Frémont named a number of peaks, rivers, and lakes after himself. Botanical tradition prohibits this particular kind of self-glorification, so when Frémont found plants that were unknown to science, he sent them to well-known botanists of the day, no doubt hoping they would commemorate him in naming the plant. This is what John Torrey did when he gave indigo bush the Latin name of *Dalea fremontii* (since changed to *Psorothamnus fremontii*).

Indigo bush thrives on gravelly plains and rocky slopes in southeastern California, northwestern Arizona and southern Nevada and Utah.

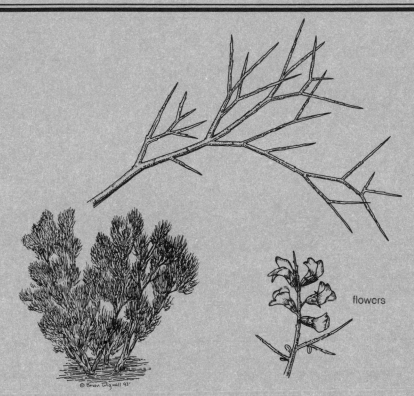

flowers

## Psorothamnus spinosus
### (A. Gray) Barnb.

Pea Family
Leguminosae

It's said that this small tree looks like a puff of smoke in a desert wash, hence the common name. Smoke tree can be found in sandy washes from southeastern California into southwestern Arizona, Baja California, and Sonora. The branches and trunks get their characteristic gray or silvery color from dense, fine hairs pressed against the stem. Each stem tip is a thorn. Leaves appear after autumn and winter rains but soon fall. Underneath their silvery coat, the stems possess abundant chlorophyll, the pigment necessary for photosynthesis, and in the absence of leaves, they produce the sugars required for growth.

The dark purple to deep blue flowers appear from late May to early July — the hottest, driest time of year. Only extreme drought can keep smoke tree from flowering. Seeds disperse in summer and germinate during the winter rainy season. This is a crucial time for the seedlings, which quickly send down deep roots into the zone of moist sand. Still, most do not survive; drought and flash floods, two ironic opposites, wipe out many seedlings before they reach maturity.

# Desert lavender

flower

*Hyptis emoryi*
**Torr.**

Mint Family
Labiatae

When rubbed between the fingers, the leaves of desert lavender smell delicious, like an old-fashioned sachet. Each tiny, violet flower has a pronounced, dipper-shaped lower lip. Clustered into heads, the faintly fragrant flowers offer nectar and attract a variety of insects, including the carpenter bee. This bulbous, black bee looks too large for such small blossoms, but by clinging to the lower lip, she gains a secure foothold while she thrusts head and tongue into the flower tube. Meanwhile, the stamens, held within the lower lip, dust her with pollen. Hummingbirds also visit the flowers but probably do not pollinate them.

Desert lavender adapts to its arid climate by changing its leaves to suit the season. When the soil is moist, the leaves are relatively large and thin, and their coat of finely branched hairs is sparse. These characteristics allow the plants to manufacture sugars at a maximum rate, taking advantage of the temporary abundance of soil moisture. As the soil dries out and temperatures climb, the plants produce smaller, thicker leaves that are gray due to a dense coat of hairs. The thicker leaves and denser hairs retard the rate of water loss. Photosynthesis slows down or comes to a complete stop as the plants adjust to arid conditions once again.

Desert lavender grows in washes and on canyon slopes in southeastern California, southwestern Arizona, and the adjacent Mexican states of Baja California and Sonora.

# Bladder sage

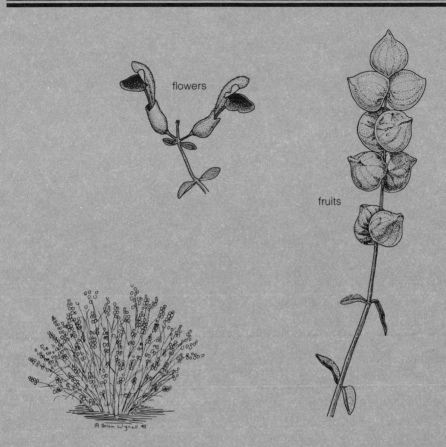

flowers

fruits

## *Salazaria mexicana*
**Torr.**

Mint Family
Labiatae

Bladder sage, also called paper-bag bush, gets its name from the fruit, which consists of four hard nutlets surrounded by a papery balloon. Derived from the calyx (the small, green cup that holds the flower), the balloon inflates as the seeds ripen, more than doubling its size. When fully expanded, the globes catch in the wind, serving as dispersal mechanisms.

The slender, flexible branches are borne in pairs along the main stems. When present, the leaves are sparse, so that the five-foot-tall shrubs seem naked and twiggy. The violet flowers appear in spring and sometimes again in autumn. They are tubular, with an upper and lower lip.

Primarily a plant of the Mojave Desert, bladder sage is found in southeastern California, southern Nevada, and northwestern Arizona. A disjunct, or widely separated, population also occurs in the Big Bend region of Texas.

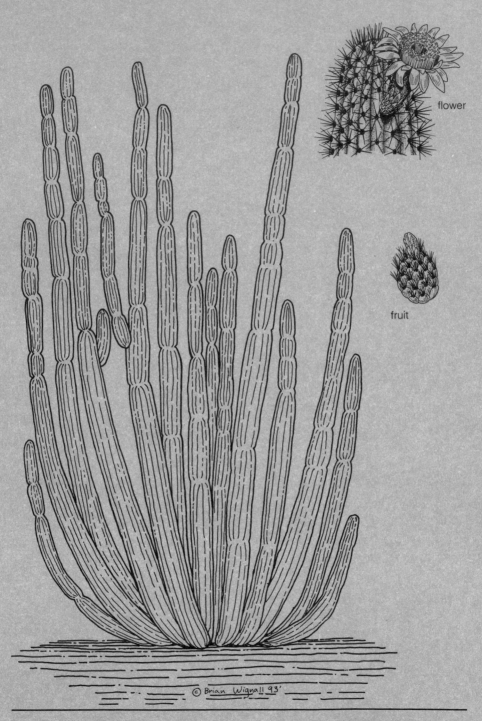

flower

fruit

© Brian Wignall 93'

# Organ pipe cactus

## Stenocereus thurberi
**(Engelm.) Buxb.**

Cactus Family
Cactaceae

How many arms does a cactus need? As many as it can get, in the case of the organ pipe. Because their surface area is small in comparison to their volume, many species of cacti, including the organ pipe, experience difficulty in manufacturing enough food to stay alive. Branching is an easy way for a cactus to increase surface area, thereby maximizing its food production.

The slender arms of organ pipe are more sensitive to cold than the massive arms of the saguaro, and, as a result, organ pipe cacti are restricted to regions where winters are mild. In Arizona, the plants typically grow on rocky slopes and cliff ledges, where nighttime radiation of heat from rocks helps protect them from frost.

Organ pipe blooms in May and June. The pale lavender flowers open shortly after sunset and close the next morning. Their night-blooming habit, musky scent, abundant nectar, and lofty placement all suggest that the flowers coevolved with bats. Indeed, nectar-feeding bats are frequent visitors. In probing the deep flower tubes for nectar, bats pollinate the blossoms. The fruits, with their abundant black seeds and sweet, red flesh, are sought by a variety of animals and insects. The Spanish common name, pitahaya dulce, or sweet pitahaya, refers to the delectable fruits.

A plant of rocky canyon slopes and hillsides, organ pipe cactus can be found in the United States only in Arizona. It is common in the southwestern corner of the state and rare at a few other, widely scattered, locations. The species is widespread in northern Mexico.

# Turpentine broom

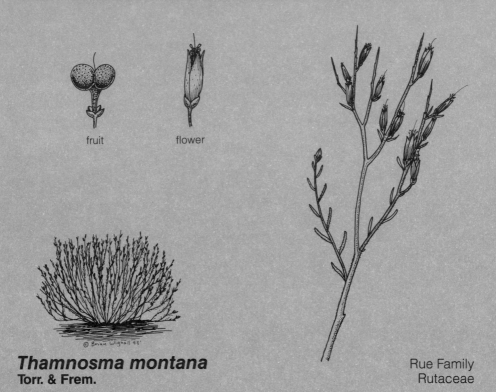

fruit

flower

***Thamnosma montana***
**Torr. & Frem.**

Rue Family
Rutaceae

Sometimes people mistake this green and usually leafless shrub for mormon tea. A quick whiff of a crushed stem will alert them to the difference: mormon tea has no particular odor; turpentine broom smells sharply and strongly like turpentine. The smell originates in the small, round glands that dot the stems. Turpentine broom belongs to the same family as the various citrus trees, and you can see similar glands on the rinds and leaves of oranges and other citrus fruits.

Caterpillars of the black swallowtail (*Papilio polyxenes coloro*), a rather large black and yellow butterfly, eat only turpentine broom. The odor of the foliage acts as a chemical signature for female black swallowtails, which lay their eggs on the foliage. By tapping the stems or leaves with their feet, the butterflies can tell the difference between turpentine broom and other plants.

This shrub flowers from January through April, one of the earliest bloomers in the desert. The deep purple flowers, stacked one above the other on the tapering, green stems, look like tiny flasks. Later in the year, the two-lobed fruits are equally conspicuous. Slender leaves appear with the flowers but fall once the soil dries out. Turpentine broom grows on rocky slopes in southeastern California, southern Nevada, and western and central Arizona.

**134**

# Suggested Reading

No field guide can include every plant in an area as rich in plant species as the Southwest. Users with some training in botany will find the following manuals indispensible for identifying Southwest trees and shrubs:

Benson, L., *The Cacti of Arizona*, Rev., 3rd ed. Tucson, Ariz.: University of Arizona Press, 1977.

Benson, L., *The Cacti of the United States and Canada*, Stanford, Calif.: Stanford University Press, 1982.

Benson, L. and R. A. Darrow, *Trees and Shrubs of the Southwestern Deserts*, 3rd ed. Tucson, Ariz.: University of Arizona Press, 1981.

Correll, D. S. and M. C. Johnston, *Manual of the Vascular Plants of Texas*, Renner, Tex.: Texas Research Foundation, 1970.

Kearney, T. H. and R. H. Peebles, *Arizona Flora*, 2nd ed., with supplement by J. T. Howell, E. McClintock and others, Berkeley, Calif.: University of California Press, 1960.

Martin, W. C. and C. R. Hutchins, *A Flora of New Mexico*, 2 vols. Monticello, La.: J Cramer, 1980.

Shreve, F. and I. L. Wiggins, *Vegetation and Flora of the Sonoran Desert*, 2 vols. Stanford, Calif.: Stanford University Press, 1964.

The discussions of desert plant ecology in this book are based on a variety of technical books and articles; too many, unfortunately, to cite individually. Readers who want to learn more about desert plant ecology will find the following books of interest:

Alcock, J., *Sonoran Desert Spring*, Chicago, Ill.: University of Chicago Press, 1986.

Alcock, J., *Sonoran Desert Summer*, Tucson, Ariz.: University of Arizona Press, 1990.

Bowers, J. E., *Seasons of the Wind: A Naturalist's Look at the Plant Life of Southwestern Sand Dunes*, Flagstaff, Ariz.: Northland Press, 1986.

Bowers, J. E., *The Mountains Next Door*, Tucson, Ariz.: University of Arizona Press, 1991.

Nabhan, G. P., *Gathering the Desert*, Tucson, Ariz.: University of Arizona Press, 1985.

Nabhan, G. P., *Saguaro: A View of Saguaro National Monument and the Tucson Basin*, Tucson, Ariz.: Southwest Parks and Monuments Association, 1986.

Zwinger, A. H., *The Mysterious Lands*, New York, N.Y.: E. P. Dutton, 1989.

# Index

NOTE: **Latin names are in bold italicized type;** *Latin family names in italicized type;* common names and English family names in regular type.

**137**

# Acknowledgments

I would like to thank the following people for taking the time to help me find and identify the plants needed to illustrate this book: Mark Dimmit, horticulturalist, Arizona-Sonora Desert Museum; Kim Stone, horticulturalist, Boyce Thompson Southwestern Arboretum; Pete Duncombe and Ray Guerra, Las Vegas Desert Demonstration Gardens; Wesley Niles, professor of botany, University of Las Vegas; author Jan Bowers for her guidance, slides, and suggestions; and my wife, Julie, for putting up with my long hours at the drawing board.

Brian Wignall